P9-DBO-054

The Elements of Teaching Writing

A Resource for Instructors
in All Disciplines

The Elements of Teaching Writing

A Resource for Instructors in All Disciplines

Katherine Gottschalk

Cornell University

Keith Hjortshoj

Cornell University

Bedford / St. Martin's   Boston ◆ New York

For Bedford/St. Martin's
Developmental Editor: Brita Mess
Production Editor: Bridget Leahy
Copyeditor: Barbara Flanagan
Text Design: Claire Seng-Niemoeller
Composition: Karla Goethe, Orchard Wind Graphics
Printing and Binding: Haddon Craftsman, an RR Donnelley & Sons Company

President: Joan E. Feinberg
Editorial Director: Denise B. Wydra
Editor in Chief: Karen S. Henry
Director of Marketing: Karen Melton Soeltz
Director of Editing, Design, and Production: Marcia Cohen
Managing Editor: Elizabeth Schaaf

Library of Congress Control Number: 2003114762

Copyright © 2004 by Bedford/St. Martins

All rights reserved. No part of this book may be reproduced, stored in a retrieval system, or transmitted in any form or by any means, electronic, mechanical, photocpying, recording, or otherwise, except as may be expressly permitted by the applicable copyright statutes or in writing by the Publisher.

Manufactured in the United States of America.

11 10 9 8

i h g

For information, write: Bedford/St. Martin's, 75 Arlington Street, Boston, MA 02116 (617-399-4000)

ISBN-10: 312–40683–5
ISBN-13: 978–0–312–40683–7

Preface

Until about twenty years ago, it was fairly safe to assume that a "writing teacher" in college was someone who taught freshman composition in an English department, using fairly consistent methods, models, and texts of a given period. According to catalogs and requirements, at least, writing instruction was almost synonymous with Freshman English.

In some ways, this identification of writing instruction with Freshman English was an illusion. Composition teachers could never fully prepare students to write effectively in their academic concentrations or career disciplines, even when the undergraduate curriculum was much less diverse and specialized than it is today. And many other teachers throughout the curriculum have always taught writing in their courses, through thoughtful assignments and comments, analysis of readings, and individual attention. We suspect that the undergraduates who become thoughtful, effective writers have always become so not just by taking a measured dose of Freshman English, but through deepening engagement and commitments, in lively association with other students and teachers, in fields of study they want to write about. This is, in our view, a timeless foundation for learning to write well and the premise on which *The Elements of Teaching Writing* is based.

Acknowledging that students learn to write—or fail to do so—throughout the curriculum, colleges and universities throughout the United States have begun to distribute responsibility for writing instruction across the curriculum as well. The majority of American colleges now include some forms of "writing across the curriculum" or "writing in the disciplines." These local developments have resulted from growing recognition that communication skills are essential to learning and to performance in every field of study, at every level of instruction, and in every profession undergraduates enter.

As a consequence of these developments, however, writing instruction now assumes a bewildering variety of forms in a comparable variety of contexts. Writing teachers, programs, methods, courses, assignments, and texts are no longer so easy to describe. When we address audiences of "writing teachers," therefore, we have several kinds of teachers and contexts in mind:

- Composition specialists in English and related fields
- A growing number of composition specialists in other fields

- Teachers of topical writing courses in their fields of study

- Teachers of designated "writing-intensive" courses in their departments

- Teachers of oral and written communication in fields such as engineering and business

- Writing program administrators who lead courses and workshops on writing instruction

- Instructors throughout the curriculum who independently assign and teach writing in their courses

Because the dimensions of writing instruction have expanded rapidly at many schools, the challenges and rewards of writing instruction are new to a large proportion of these teachers. Graduate teaching assistants assigned to writing or writing-intensive courses in their fields are typically new to college teaching in general and find that writing instruction further complicates responsibilities that are already mysterious and complex. Because training in college teaching is rarely a component of graduate education, except through trial and error, newly appointed faculty members are often assigned to types of courses they have no experience designing and teaching. These courses might include seminars with extensive writing and discussion or larger classes that satisfy requirements in a writing-across-the-curriculum program. When they begin to teach writing or writing-intensive courses in their fields, experienced college teachers often find themselves in new territory as well. They quickly learn that this venture does not end with the addition of a couple of writing assignments to last year's syllabus. At the very least they must read, respond to, and evaluate this writing. And if they want to integrate this writing with learning and improve the quality of the papers they assign, they must continue to change their courses and teaching methods.

As directors of First-Year Writing Seminars and Writing in the Majors in the Knight Institute for Writing in the Disciplines at Cornell University, we have worked closely with teachers in all of these circumstances and others, across a wide range of disciplines, course designs, and levels of instruction. *How can I teach writing in my course?* is the complex question we hear most often and spend most of our time trying to answer. For this purpose we cannot reduce *The Elements of Teaching Writing* to a list of rules everyone should follow. From our experiences at Cornell alone, detailed answers to this question would fill several large volumes and would vary considerably from one course and field of study to another.[1]

---

[1]For those wishing to learn more about the Knight Institute for Writing in the Disciplines and the cultures of writing at Cornell, two volumes have recently become available. Edited by Jonathan Monroe, the Knight Institute's director, *Writing and Revising the Disciplines* is a volume of reflections by professors in the physical sciences, social sciences, and humanities. Also edited by Monroe is *Local Knowledges, Local Practices: Writing in the Disciplines at Cornell,* in which faculty in the Knight Institute's programs share their pedagogical techniques, insights, and aspirations.

In our collaboration with teachers of writing in the disciplines, however, certain issues arise with great consistency. To address these issues more efficiently, over the years we have produced a variety of materials we can distribute to teachers and use in our courses and workshops on teaching writing. And for some time we have wanted to condense this material into a small book that would answer the most common questions teachers ask about writing instruction, lead them toward answers of their own, or help them evaluate methods they currently use. With the virtue of brevity in mind, we have condensed the "key elements" of each (brief) chapter into introductory lists of suggestions. These condensed points can serve as references to the full passages in the text, as quick overview of the topic, or as reminders of central ideas after reading the chapter.

These "elements of teaching writing" represent the redistribution of understandings and strategies we have gathered from hundreds of colleagues, at Cornell and at other institutions. These resources include our colleagues in the Knight Institute for Writing in the Disciplines, faculty and graduate students in many departments at Cornell, participants in the Knight Consortium for Writing in the Disciplines each summer, and teachers of writing at many other institutions. We are grateful to all of these people, too numerous to list individually, for their contributions to this book.

We are also deeply grateful to the publishers and editors at Bedford/St. Martin's for getting the project off the ground and into print. The basic idea of the book took shape at a lively meeting with Chuck Christensen, Joan Feinberg, and Karen Henry. Karen Henry, Brita Mess, Bridget Leahy, and Barbara Flanagan at Bedford have skillfully steered us through drafts and revisions. Many of these revisions were inspired by exceptionally helpful reviews of the manuscript, from John Forester, Ejner Jensen, James Slevin, and Sharon Williams.

Contents

9 Strategies for Including Writing in Large Courses 145

10 Teaching as a Work in Progress 162

Conclusion National Implications, Local Practices 168

Some Basic Questions and Answers

Teachers throughout the college curriculum have always assigned and evaluated student writing. In recent decades, however, distribution of responsibility for writing instruction across the curriculum has led teachers in all fields of study to question what they can do to improve student writing and other communication skills, at least in their own courses and concentrations. How can they compose more effective assignments, provide better comments and guidance, engage students in investigative writing projects, encourage stronger reading skills, and foster the kinds of discussion and thinking from which sharply focused, interesting writing emerges? *The Elements of Teaching Writing* represents our attempt to answer these specific questions. And these answers — presented as analyses of the central problems and strategies for solving them — come not just from us, but indirectly from the hundreds of teachers we have known who have developed innovative methods of assigning, evaluating, and improving student writing in a great variety of courses and disciplines.

Underlying these matters of approach and practice, however, are some more fundamental questions that writing teachers and program administrators often prefer to avoid, because they are both controversial and difficult to answer. Yet differing answers to these hard questions, or confusion about them, can have profound influences on the roles and responsibilities teachers assume, on their views of student writing, and on their teaching practices. Tempting as it is to dodge them, therefore, we will begin with a few of the most basic questions teachers ask. Our replies establish some of the conceptual foundations on which further chapters are based.

What Is Wrong with Student Writing?
(And Who Is Responsible?)

Everyone who directs a college writing program has heard frequent complaints from other teachers about the quality of student writing:

> *My students don't write or think clearly.*
>
> *They don't know how to present an argument.*
>
> *They don't know how to state and support a thesis.*
>
> *They don't know how to use and document sources.*
>
> *They don't know how to read critically and analytically.*
>
> *They didn't follow the assignment.*
>
> *They don't revise and proofread their papers.*
>
> *They haven't learned the basics of grammar and composition.*

The prevalence of such criticism and disappointment suggests that most college teachers believe that student writing is worse than it should be, and perhaps worse than it used to be. Along with their dissatisfaction we often hear theories of degeneration, caused by television, some say, by computers, or by other trends in popular culture. The weakness of student writing is often linked with a decline in reading, with the deterioration of secondary education, or with the growing emphasis on standardized testing. Teachers in advanced courses often hold freshman composition teachers responsible for the problems they observe in student papers, and freshman writing teachers often blame secondary schools. Whatever students can't or don't do well in a history, sociology, or economics assignment, they *should* have learned, teachers say, in their freshman writing courses, if not in high school English. Our colleagues in other departments express genuine bewilderment when they ask students to take positions, for example, and receive passive summaries of the assigned readings. *In their freshman writing courses, don't they learn what an argument is?* these teachers ask.

In response, we will not argue that college students are, on the whole, good writers whose work should satisfy their teachers. In our own classes and in others, we have seen too many shallow, disjointed, error-ridden, and generally misbegotten papers to dismiss the kinds of criticism listed at the beginning of this introduction. When teachers show us examples of poor writing from their classes, their perceptions of the shortcomings in student papers are usually accurate, and the qualities they find missing are important. We rarely tell them that they should lower their standards or ignore the problems they observe.

Does this mean that student writing skills have deteriorated? Probably not. Owing to complex changes in demographics, standards, and curricula, stable criteria for tracking the quality of student writing are difficult if not impossible to define. But there is little evidence that undergraduate writing has worsened since the first writing assessments of entering students at Harvard in 1874, which half of the freshmen failed even though the criteria for passing were, by today's standards, quite low. Describing this dismal performance in an address to secondary school teachers in 1879, Adams Sherman Hill, a Harvard graduate and professor, noted that in addition to atrocious punctuation and spelling (even of words included in the examination questions), failing exams "were deformed by grossly ungrammatical or profoundly obscure sentences, and some by absolute illiteracy" (Brereton 50). The half of the compositions that did pass were, from Hill's perspective, still afflicted by deficiencies strikingly familiar to college teachers today. And like many college teachers in following decades, Hill leveled much of the blame for these weaknesses at teachers in secondary schools:

> The great majority of the compositions this year, as in previous years, were characterized by general defects, which, though not taken into account by the examiner, point to grave imperfections in the method (or want of a method) of the preparatory schools. The suggestions at the head of the paper were often disregarded in the letter, and almost always in the spirit. The candidate, instead of considering what he had to say and arranging his thoughts before beginning to write, either wrote without thinking about the matter at all, or thought to no purpose. Instead of aiming at good work, and to that end subjecting his composition to careful revision, he either did not undertake to revise at all, or did not know how to correct his errors. Evidently he had never been taught the value of previous thought or of subsequent criticism. (50–51)

Given the detail and gravity of Hill's criticism, it is hard to imagine greater disappointment with the quality of student writing or further deterioration of language skills over the next century.

Following developments at Harvard in the 1870s, writing assessments and freshman composition requirements gradually became standard features of higher education throughout the country. With this growing emphasis on writing skills, we might expect to see corresponding improvement in undergraduate writing. But two other factors sustained the perception, at least, of weakness or even deterioration.

One was the expansion and increasing diversity of the undergraduate population — an expansion that has continued to enrich and to challenge higher education to the present, now that 63 percent of high school graduates attend college. Perhaps it is most useful to think of periodic crises and ongoing concern over the language skills of undergraduates as manifestations of necessary, awkward, and sometimes reluctant adjustment to changes in undergraduate populations and their needs. For decades, growing staffs of composition specialists have struggled to meet these needs with a great variety of teaching strategies, along with assessment programs, tiered courses for students with different skills and backgrounds, ESL classes, campus writing centers, peer tutoring programs, and other services.

Yet a second factor continually challenges both students and teachers of writing: the increasing variety and specialization of undergraduate studies. We can at least imagine the possibility of teaching a uniform set of expository writing skills to meet the demands of a liberal education in the nineteenth century — a vision that created freshman composition requirements. Today, however, students from a great variety of linguistic backgrounds face a bewildering variety of writing tasks, in preparation for highly specialized careers. In their diverse undergraduate courses and majors they must complete particular kinds of lab reports, case studies, research papers, proposals, literature reviews, memos, arguments, interpretations, historical narratives, impact statements, and essay questions based on different sources of information and specific professional models. These forms and standards can change dramatically from one level of instruction to the next, even in a single department.

Against this background we can answer the first of our questions.

What is wrong with student writing?

For some students, poor writing results from a weak grasp of written English in general, resulting from inadequate instruction or the use of English as a foreign language. On the whole, however, disappointment with the quality of student writing results from two other factors that teachers can address in their courses:

- Unfamiliarity with the assigned task

- Inappropriate methods (or lack of time) for completing the task successfully

In the majority of their assignments, in other words, undergraduates are trying to do a particular kind of writing for the first time, often without models or adequate guidance. Learning to write well is therefore a continual process of trial and error in which rules and expectations unpredictably change. Close deadlines, congested schedules, procrastination, and previous habits can lead the great majority of these students to try to complete an assignment in a single draft, often on the night before it is due. We shouldn't be surprised, then, if writers who are trying to do something unfamiliar, without much preparation or revision, don't get it right. Considering these circumstances and methods, it is more surprising when they produce even rough approximations of the work we had in mind.

Who is responsible for improving student writing?

All of us, including student writers themselves. Like other writers, college students are ultimately responsible for the work they produce, even under difficult circumstances, and we cannot improve student writing by placing this burden entirely on the shoulders of teachers.

But teachers are always implicated in the writing their students produce. In our assignments we construct occasions for writing, purposes, time frames, and guidelines. We are the primary audiences for their work, which we evaluate according to our own criteria and expectations. Because student writers are trying to do what we ask them to do, the quality of their work results in part from the contexts we create and the guidance we provide. The skill, effort, and attention individual students devote to the task will vary in ways we can't entirely control. But we can improve the general quality of student writing and the quality of their learning experiences by creating contexts that give our students the opportunity, at least, to meet their responsibilities more effectively.

Who Am I to Teach Writing?

When you decide to teach a course in your field that is designated "writing-intensive," teach a topical writing course in your field, or simply want to improve assignments and papers in your classes, you may start out with the idea that writing instruction is something other than or in addition to the kind of teaching you would normally do. Teaching writing will appear to be something other than teaching philosophy, evolutionary biology, or microeconomics. And to the extent that you deliver writing instruction, you might imagine that you should do what professional writing teachers do for their purposes, to raise the level of undergraduate writing skills. For that purpose, you would need to become a kind of teacher you do not happen to be — to adopt goals you do not already try to meet, with expertise you do not yet possess.

It is true, as we have noted, that formal writing instruction has traditionally occurred in a particular kind of course, designed to improve the general writing skills of an increasingly diverse undergraduate population. As these freshman courses and requirements became standard features of the undergraduate curriculum, primarily within departments of English, teaching writing also became a profession unto itself, distinct from the teaching of literature, history, biology, and other disciplines. In such courses, assigned readings and discussions on diverse topics are occasions for writing, which is the primary focus of attention. And because students write and revise several papers, with extensive feedback from the teacher, the typical writing class is small — fifteen to twenty students — and taught in a seminar format. Over the decades, writing teachers have developed a wide range of strategies for delivering this special type of instruction, strategies exchanged in professional journals and conferences.

But this kind of course and teacher was never meant to replace writing instruction in the disciplines; nor was it entirely separate from academic concentrations. Historically, the people who taught freshman composition were formally trained in literary studies, not in writing instruction per se. This is why early composition courses were essentially literature classes and why those of us who satisfied writing requirements in such courses still think of writing as "English" (and of writing teachers as "English teachers") even if all the writing we do is in another field. Extensive graduate programs for writing instruction (or "rhetoric and composition") are fairly recent developments, still within the field of English.

Real writing instruction has always occurred in other fields, contexts, and forms, in courses of all sizes and at all levels throughout the curriculum — wherever teachers take active measures to help their students write effectively. In this respect, writing instruction is just a kind of thoughtful attention to uses of language, in your course and field of study and in the written work you assign. Real writing instruction can and should be integral to your own goals for teaching and learning and should utilize your own expertise. As we will explain in later chapters, this instruction is often simply a matter of making your own knowledge and expectations explicit, in terms of the forms, functions, and methods of writing you assign.

As a consequence, "thoughtful attention" is essential, and while teaching writing is not just a specialized form of instruction, we should emphasize that it is not just a matter of assigning and grading writing either. A brief example will illustrate what we mean by thoughtful, strategic attention to uses of written language in a course, in ways that utilize your own expertise.

One of our students recently told us with dismay that his professor in an introductory business course was very disappointed with the papers he had assigned on a case study of corporate development. This assignment, due in one week, simply asked students to read the case, identify a specific challenge the company would face in coming years, and make recommendations for meeting that challenge. The resulting papers were so terrible that this professor spent the next lecture period angrily explaining to his students what they did wrong and what they should have done instead.

This teacher might also have asked himself what *he* did wrong and what *he* should have done instead. Analyses of cases are standard writing assignments in business programs, but few of the students in this introductory class had ever written one. High school and freshman composition teachers can't prepare students for such specialized assignments, and there is no reason to assume that students can accurately reproduce the genre of a case study without guidance. This business professor obviously knew and could explain the kind of writing he expected. If he had provided explanations and examples in advance, the assignment might have become a more positive, successful learning experience that raised, rather than lowered, the students' morale and motivation. This change would not have consumed more class time, and the task of reading and evaluating student papers might have become more efficient and less frustrating.

From our perspective, this change would represent one kind of shift from simply assigning writing to teaching writing: actively thinking about the type of writing assigned, considering what students need to learn in order to complete that assignment successfully, and providing the appropriate instruction. This kind of writing instruction doesn't require the importation of knowledge and skills from some other discipline. In fact, people in other fields, including professional composition teachers, are unlikely to possess the knowledge and skills this teaching requires.

In response to the question *Who am I to teach writing?*, therefore, we might ask another: *For your course and field of study, who else is going to teach writing if you don't?*

What Is Good Writing?

This hard question is closely related to previous ones and is perhaps fundamental to them. If we perceive that something is wrong with student writing, we must be able to recognize better writing when we see it, even if we can't precisely explain the differences. And if we set out to teach writing, to improve the quality of student work, we should know what improvement means: what good writing (or at least better writing) should look like. This question is also related to the notion that writing instruction is something other than the teaching we would normally do — a kind of knowledge and skill that other kinds of teachers possess. *Real* writing teachers, from this perspective, should know more clearly what good writing is and how it comes about. If the rest of us aren't entirely sure what good writing is — aren't even sure, therefore, that we are good writers ourselves — how can we effectively teach and evaluate writing in our courses?

This issue remains just as contentious and unresolved among composition specialists, however, as it is for everyone else. Even E. B. White, a paragon of literary virtue, concluded his and William Strunk's book of rules for good writing, *The Elements of Style*, with the suggestion that the qualities that produce stylistic excellence are ultimately mysterious. While we can't entirely lay this issue to rest, we can illuminate some of its constituent arguments, along with the positions on which the following chapters are based.

From our discussions with teachers and students, we observe three very different conceptions of good writing, each with its own implications:

- The belief that there are universal features of good writing that apply to all forms and fields of discourse

- The belief that criteria for good writing differ from one context, genre, or "discourse community" to another, to the extent that good writing in one course or field of study might represent bad writing in another

- The belief that qualities of good writing are in the eye of the beholder and are therefore entirely subjective

To put our own cards on the table quickly, we don't believe that any of these positions is entirely valid, though each contains some truth.

For example, the assertion that there are universal features of good writing is useless until we determine what those features are, and such explanation usually takes the form of lists of general traits, such as *correctness, clarity*, and *cohesion*. While each of these features might be necessary, none is sufficient. All good writing is grammatically correct, perhaps, but writing that is perfectly correct can still be awkward, boring, or incoherent. Adding more features, as qualifications, we still end up with an incomplete list of general, descriptive terms — not really a working definition, much less an explanation.

And the ambiguities of this first position quickly lead us to the second. When a generalist asserts, for example, *All good writing should be clear*, the skeptic asks, *Clear to whom? To everyone?* In reference to academic writing, we can't easily ignore these questions. An article in a publication such as the *Journal of Mathematical Physics*, for example, or those in some branches of linguistics or literary theory, will be quite opaque to most scholars in unrelated fields and to the general public. Does this mean that good writing is impossible in highly specialized professions or that criteria for good writing and clarity are defined within those communities of writers?

If we adopt the latter position, however, we run up against the fact that the boundaries of such communities are impossible to define with any precision, especially for the purpose of teaching writing. Academic departments do not constitute homogeneous communities of writers. People within them often write in a great variety of forms and styles, according to differing criteria that are often interdisciplinary. Particular psychologists, for example, might produce "good writing" that closely resembles writing done in neurobiology, information science, or sociology. And to the extent that these departments or interdisciplinary fields represent literary communities, undergraduates are not necessarily members of them. The writing that teachers assign to students is often very different from the writing they produce for their peers as scholars, and standards for evaluation differ accordingly.

So this argument devolves to the third, relativistic position: that features of good writing are matters of individual preference and perception that can depend even on the reader's mood at the moment. Moods, perceptions, and standards can change, for example, through the process of evaluating a large number of student papers on the same assignment. The belief that the evaluation of writing is "subjective" can severely undermine the will and confidence of teachers who want to assign writing but doubt their ability to evaluate student work fairly and bring about improvements of any lasting value. These doubts are especially common among teachers accustomed to "objective" measures of quantitative and factual knowledge.

The seemingly arbitrary standards for evaluating written work can afflict student writers as well, especially if they feel that every teacher is using a different set of hidden criteria. "It's all luck," one undergraduate concluded:

I used to think I was a good writer, but now I don't know. Sometimes I work for days on a paper, and the teacher hates it. Sometimes I whip it off in a couple of hours and it turns out great. Maybe it's my mood. Maybe it's the teacher. I don't know. It's always a gamble, so I avoid writing whenever I can, and when I can't avoid it I just do it, and see what happens.

To the extent that our criteria for evaluating student writing are peculiar to individual assignments, courses, and disciplines, therefore, we need to make those criteria as clear to our students as possible before they write. Much of the confusion and avoidance this student describes resulted from failure to make these expectations clear, often because teachers falsely assume (from the first position we listed) that their own standards for good writing are universal.

Because the challenge of adapting to differing standards represents an essential form of learning in all fields, furthermore, we do not serve our students well by avoiding this issue in our teaching practices. If undergraduates who pursue a subject into graduate studies do not encounter conflicting standards and evaluations of writing among their courses, they will face that reality among peer reviews of the first manuscript they submit for publication in any field, including the sciences and mathematics.

Because you are the primary audience for the writing you assign, therefore, you need to let students know what *you* consider good writing to be for these occasions. But we also believe that these criteria for good writing are to varying degrees collective and in a few ways very general, at least for academic writing and especially for student writing.

As stories about research, for example, good scientific reports follow a basic sequence of connected sections that we can think of as answers to a series of questions:

- *What were we investigating and why?*

- *How did we pursue this investigation?*

- *What did we find out?*

- *What do these results mean?*

Language, often supplemented by figures and equations, moves fluently through this basic form, which is used throughout the sciences and in many social sciences as well. As George Gopen and Judith Swan explain in "The Science of Scientific Writing" (published in a 1990 issue of *American Scientist*), a good scientific report conveys its substance in ways that accommodate the highly structured, collective expectations of readers. These expectations include not only the broad sequence of sections just listed but also the organization of information within sections, paragraphs, sentences, graphs, and tables. Gopen and Swan note, for example, that readers expect important information to land in "stress positions," usually at the beginning and end of sections, paragraphs, or sentences. A good report sustains reading through these structures and also allows readers to find information easily in predictable locations. Because undergraduates, as a rule, are not aware of these structures and expectations, making them explicit will clarify your standards along with some broader standards useful in other courses. And this clarification *is* the teaching of writing.

Some of these observations about a particular kind of writing, the scientific report, carry over to more general conceptions of good writing as well. Over the years, we have asked scholars in a variety of fields to give us examples of what they consider good writing in their own areas of specialization, varying from English and history to chemistry and physics. Of course the styles, forms, audiences, and purposes of this professional literature vary considerably.[1] But we could also observe some general features that these selected examples of good writing hold in common:

- The writing is "voiced." In other words, as readers we sense the presence of a writer writing, addressing us, taking responsibility for our understanding and, in effect, ushering us through the text. This sense of voice does not rely on first- and second-person address (*I . . . you*), but the writers often use cues and transitions to maintain and direct attention.

- While these are typically dispassionate voices of reason and explanation (not chatty or personal), they are also relaxed and engaged with the subject — not excessively formal or detached. The authors are writing with a pleasing combination of authority and composure.

- The authors use this authority and composure to make difficult subjects easier for us to understand, not to demonstrate the complexity and difficulty of their knowledge (a common mistake among student writers and scholars).

- The organization and flow of the writing sustains continuous reading from a *point of departure*, in a *clear direction*, toward a *destination*. The writing supports this continuous, directed movement and does not let us down with disconnections, unexpected turns, or loops that force us to read back over previous sections.

These qualities of good writing are evident even among research articles in highly specialized fields, intended for audiences of specialists, but they are more apparent in student writing submitted for awards in our interdisciplinary programs. When we read the best of these pa-

---

[1]In the chapter "What Written Knowledge Does" in his book *Shaping Written Knowledge,* Charles Bazerman analyzes many of these differences in three examples of professional writing in biology, the sociology of science, and literary studies.

pers, we encounter the same qualities of composure and engagement. These essays also sustain continuous reading from a clear point of departure, in a clear direction, toward a real destination. The best of them, in other words, don't let us down as readers.

Like the best professional articles, each of these student essays serves specific purposes within a specific field of study, according to criteria spelled out in the assignments students submit to us with their papers. Great writing for one course would not necessarily impress teachers in another, and two teachers even in the same field might evaluate the same paper somewhat differently. If the qualities of good writing were entirely subjective, however, or wholly confined to specific courses and fields of study, we would have no basis for comparing and reaching agreement about their strengths and weaknesses. Nor could these student writers reliably transport their skills from one field of study to another. But they do, as we have learned from getting to know many of these student writers. And if there are skills and qualities they can transport from one course to another, there are also valuable writing skills and qualities we can teach in accordance with the goals of specific fields of study.

1

Integrating Writing and Learning in Your Course Design

Key Elements

Elements   14

We intend that the term *elements* have two meanings:

- Some *basic, fundamental* considerations for teaching writing throughout the curriculum
- The potential *components* or *constituent elements* of effective writing instruction

In this chapter we emphasize the first of these meanings, discussing some basic approaches to the design of effective courses along with some fundamental conceptions and misconceptions that influence the inclusion or exclusion of writing in plans for teaching.

Writing vs. Content: A False Dichotomy   14

As a result of the differing conceptions of writing courses and content courses, the goals of teaching writing and teaching content might appear to conflict. When teachers treat writing as a separate component of a course, students perceive assignments to be disconnected from learning even when these assignments are vitally connected with learning the subject. Dissonance occurs when the goals of writing and the goals of learning appear to be at odds.

Ideally, we should be able to design courses that put writing into solution with learning and content, a synthesis that has its foundations in the realities of teaching and learning.

A Typical Syllabus Is Not a Course Design 18

One of the best reasons for integrating writing with learning is to give students time, reasons, and opportunities for understanding complex subjects: making connections among ideas and readings, grasping concepts they can use for further understanding, and thinking critically about the course material. To a great extent, through carefully planned assignments and activities, you can create the kinds of learning experiences that correspond with your teaching goals. You can think of this approach to course design as a series of related questions:

- In what ways do I want students to learn this subject?
- What kinds of writing, reading, speaking, and listening will elicit these kinds of learning and requisite skills?
- What kinds of information do I need to provide — in lectures, assigned readings, instructions, and other course materials — to support these learning activities?

Knowledge and Inquiry:
Two Models of Scholarship and Teaching 21

1. We can view teaching as an opportunity to tell students what we know about a subject.
2. We can view teaching as an opportunity to engage students in the kinds of inquiry — and thus in the kinds of thinking and learning — we pursue.

If students believe that learning is knowing in a course, they will also believe that writing is not a medium of inquiry and exchange but a medium for demonstrating knowledge: a kind of take-home exam. This is why we recommend that for the purpose of assigning and teaching writing in your discipline you should base your course design not on the body of content students should know but on the questions you want to raise, with plenty of occasions for students to raise questions of their own. You can think of teaching as research into the ways in which students actually learn this material. You can think of your course, therefore, as an ongoing experiment.

Writing, Reading, Speaking, and Listening
for Active Learning 24

As an instrument of learning and inquiry, writing can take many forms, in conjunction with other uses of language. In a course that emphasizes active learning, these diverse forms of writing fall into place naturally, in lively interconnection with speaking, listening, and reading.

Safety First: Establishing Structure, Rules, and Standards 26

If students feel safe in a class, they will participate in unfamiliar activities and even help to make those activities work; if students do not feel safe in a class, they will be reluctant even to speak.

The most lively, productive interaction in classes usually results from clearly structured guidelines. Unstructured classes and undirected activities can in fact seem the most hazardous to students, because from one moment to the next they do not know what is going to happen to them.

Elements

From our long experience with interdisciplinary programs, at Cornell and many other schools, we know that there are very few consistent features of college courses. Even in a single college or university, the undergraduate curriculum includes courses that differ radically in size, subject, function, level, and learning goals; and these variations increase when we compare a small liberal arts college, for example, with a large research university. Given these variations, a crisp definition of a writing course is possible only if we confine such courses to a specific corner of the curriculum.

Because we believe that forms of writing instruction can be productively integrated with learning in the great majority of undergraduate courses and fields of study, we don't pretend that we can tell you exactly how a writing or writing-intensive course should be designed: how much writing or revision you should assign, the forms these assignments should take, how much time you should plan to devote to them, their purposes in your course, or how writing should be integrated with subject matter in your field. The specific answers to these questions will depend on many factors we can't predict. And because in our own programs we encourage the invention of writing instruction in as many forms and contexts as possible, we can't prescribe a template for course design without contradicting our own goals and commitments.

In the remaining chapters of this book, we will instead describe and explain a great variety of "elements" you can potentially include in your course plans and teaching, according to your own goals and circumstances.

For this purpose we intend that the term *elements* have two meanings:

- Some *basic*, *fundamental* considerations for teaching writing throughout the curriculum

- The potential *components* or *constituent elements* of effective writing instruction

In this chapter on course design, we will emphasize the first of these meanings and discuss some basic approaches to the design of effective courses, along with some fundamental conceptions and misconceptions that influence the inclusion or exclusion of writing in plans for teaching. These views result from our observation that fixed assumptions established early in the course design process can make potentially good ideas seem irrelevant or unfeasible. In other words, the suggestions we offer in further chapters will not seem applicable to your teaching if your initial approach to course design excludes them.

Writing vs. Content: A False Dichotomy

The common distinction between "writing" and "content" results in part from the form (and, for most of us, the memory) of traditional writing courses that use subject matter for the central purpose of teaching writing skills. When they design such courses, writing teachers choose readings or issues that will provide material for specific kinds of writing, which is the main object of instruction. Textbooks designed for these courses usually contain readings on a variety of topics, from diverse sources and disciplines. And while they might focus on a particular kind of essay, such as argument, these books and courses do not attempt to cover a particular field of inquiry. As an object of instruction, therefore, writing seems separable from subject matter, or "content."

By contrast, teachers in specific fields of study usually think of a course as a body of subject matter — information, concepts, or issues — they hope to cover during the term. The syllabus for such a course usually takes the form of a topical sequence, with related readings and other assignments that help to convey the information the teacher hopes to cover in specific periods. If general textbooks for the course are available, they are similarly organized for topical and categorical coverage of the subject. Assigned writing usually serves to test the students' grasp of this material.

As a result of these differing conceptions of a course, the goals of "teaching writing" and "teaching content" might appear to conflict. If you initially think of a course in terms of the subject matter you hope to cover during the term, that "content" will quickly fill out your syllabus. Once that view of the course is established, including writing, writing instruction, and related activities will seem to add an alien substance that displaces content, like dropping a stone into a bucket already filled with water.

Facing the prospect of teaching a writing or writing-intensive course in their fields, therefore, instructors often ask, *How can I find room for writing in my class without sacrificing content?*

Or, thinking of writing instruction as some other kind of teaching, they ask, *How can I teach writing and teach American history (or nutrition or cognitive psychology) in the same class?*

Institutional mandates for teaching writing "across the curriculum" or "in the disciplines" often appear to create the dilemma inherent in these questions. They seem to ask teachers in the disciplines to share the burden of doing what traditional writing teachers do, by *adding* writing assignments and instruction to the content of their courses. Instructors who try to live up to this expectation therefore feel they must teach writing *on top of* teaching history or economics, spend time teaching writing *on the side,* or *find room for writing* in their courses. All of these phrases presume that the goals and methods of teaching writing are distinct from the real substance of a course and thus compete for time and attention with the teaching of content.

As most instructors soon discover, this dichotomy rarely works in practice, for teachers or for students. If teachers simply add writing assignments and instruction to the existing design of a course, they create more work for themselves and for their students. If they try to teach writing on the side of teaching substance, that work tends to become sidelined: marginal and less substantial. If they try to make room for writing instruction with a cut-and-paste approach, they feel they have sacrificed important content and reduced the substance of the course.

And when students perceive that writing assignments are added to or encapsulated within the real content of a course, they tend to view these assignments as additional burdens, of marginal relevance to learning the subject. From student evaluations we have found that when teachers treat writing as a separate component of a course, students perceive assignments to be disconnected from learning even when these assignments are vitally connected with learning the subject.

Two Examples

In an economic theory course for majors in the field, Robert Frank assigned two papers that asked students to think and write as "economic naturalists": "to use a principle, or principles, discussed in the course to explain some pattern of events or behavior that you personally have observed." Frank designed these assignments to give students an empirical basis, a grounding in their own experience, for understanding and criticizing theories they would otherwise learn (or not learn) as abstract formulations.

Although the topics students chose were of direct interest to them (e.g., the pricing of rock concert tickets or the implications of utility costs in apartment leases) and of direct relevance to the subject of the course, in the first year Frank introduced these papers and the TA-led discussion sessions as occasions for writing instruction, affiliated with Cornell's writing programs. In their written course evaluations, most students said the writing assignments and/or discussions of writing were of little relevance to their understanding of the course content. Some equated this work, negatively, with taking freshman writing classes.

The following year, Frank and the same teaching assistant used the same assignments with added revisions, but they did not distinguish this writing or the discussion sessions from the study of economics. Students were more engaged with the assignments, their papers were better than those of the previous year, and they considered the assignments directly relevant to learning economics. Asked in a numerical evaluation "How well did the writing assignments contribute to your understanding of the course material?" students responded with an average of 4.3 on a scale of 1 to 5. (In ways we will describe in Chapter 9, Frank later adapted these "economic naturalist" assignments for use in a very large microeconomics course, with about four hundred students.)

Asked why they chose a writing-intensive, extra-credit section of a course on evolution for biology majors, all but one student in the class said that they learned the material more thoroughly and deeply through papers and revisions, debates, field studies, and student-led discussions in this alternative to regular discussion sections and exams. Although they were writing constantly throughout the term, they did not distinguish this writing and the extensive guidance on their assignments from learning evolutionary biology. (Nor did the sixty biology majors who signed a petition to the department requesting more of these popular options.) The one exception explained that he came to college with two main goals: to become a biologist and to become a professional writer. He thought he would have to pursue these goals separately, but in this class he found that he could pursue both at once.

These examples and other evidence indicate that writing assignments and instruction are most effective when they are fully integrated with learning and content in a field of study. And this premise applies as well to the traditional composition class, where writing itself is the primary subject of the course. In such classes students do not experience conflict between writing and learning because writing is, explicitly, what they are supposed to learn. Dissonance occurs when the goals of writing and the goals of learning appear to be at odds.

Ideally, therefore, we should be able to design courses that put writing into solution with learning and content. Writing, in such a course, would not be separate from learning about forest ecology, Greek drama, or American foreign policy. Teaching writing would not be different from teaching these and other subjects; and attention to writing would not displace the substance of a course, because writing would be a way of learning and communicating ideas about the subject at hand.

This ideal synthesis of writing and content has foundations in the realities of teaching and learning:

- *The real "content" of a course can't be clearly distinguished from the written and spoken language through which this content is conveyed.* Almost all teaching and learning occurs through varieties of verbal activity: writing, reading, speaking, or listening. This statement holds true even for courses that emphasize visual or mathematical representation or "hands-on" experience. Regardless of the subjects you teach, imagine teaching without written or spoken language. How much "content" would be left?

- *Writing and other communication skills are essential for performance in every field of study and in every career undergraduates enter.* Graduate programs and employers commonly rank written and oral communication skills as their highest priorities for candidates, above specialized knowledge. It seems reasonable that the communication skills most important to a field of study should be essential to learning that subject.

- *The language and learning skills students use in a course constitute an important, lasting dimension of their education.* An essential part of what students learn in a course is *how* to learn in that course, and they usually retain and utilize these learning strategies well beyond memory of factual information. Almost all of these learning skills are also language skills, to varying degrees *passive* (listening to lectures and taking notes), *active* (writing a position paper), or *interactive* (participating in discussions or collaborative projects).

A Typical Syllabus Is Not a Course Design

In practice, every course emphasizes certain kinds of language skills over others, and these uses of language largely determine the kinds of learning that occur. When they plan courses and compose syllabi with primary concern for coverage, teachers usually do not take these dimensions of learning deliberately into account; but written and spoken language are still constantly at work, influencing the kinds of knowledge and skills students develop.

Even in a lecture course that does not include formal writing assignments or discussion periods, teachers speak during lectures, write on the board, produce written handouts and other course materials, assign readings, and read student work, such as exams; students listen to lectures, write notes to record information, and read assigned texts and other material to understand lectures and prepare for exams, which probably require some writing as well.

All of these uses of language and others (such as conversations and e-mail messages about the course) heavily determine — probably more than the categories of information on the syllabus do — what the students will actually get out of the class: its real "content." And for a variety of reasons, this real content does not reliably correspond with the ideas and information teachers hope to cover in a conventional lecture course. The fact that lectures and assigned readings cover a topic on your syllabus does not mean your students will learn this material in the way you intend.

Educational research indicates that many factors, all related to language use, limit amounts and types of learning:

- Even if they are alert, students are not able to sustain attention to continuous lectures beyond ten or fifteen minutes at a time. They are most attentive at the beginning and end of a lecture period and most likely to miss information in the middle.

- Partly because they have to write and listen at once, attentive students typically record less than half of the most important information and ideas in a lecture.

- If they have not recorded this material in a form that will restore understanding, students will quickly forget most of what they learned in class.

- This weakness of short-term memory applies also to reading. Unless students write notes or papers about reading assignments or talk about them in discussions, they will quickly forget most of what they read.

- If they are trying to record and recall large amounts of material, students are most likely to miss the *connections* among facts, concepts, and viewpoints. Analysis, synthesis, critical thinking, the application of concepts to new cases, and other complex forms of learning all conflict to some extent with the goals of extensive coverage.

When their attention drifts from a lecture, for example, students are not necessarily daydreaming. Sometimes they are still thinking about what you just said: trying to grasp what it means, relate it to their own experience, connect this idea with other dimensions of the course, or resolve doubts about its validity. These further thoughts are potentially relevant, perhaps even crucial, to their understanding. Yet if the train of coverage continues to barrel down the track, toward the next topic on the syllabus, students will feel that this kind of reflection is irrelevant or even disruptive to the kind of learning you expect. Brilliant observations, points of contention, and matters of confusion will be functionally extraneous and in most cases forgotten by the next class period.

A colleague in political science, for example, once asked her students to write summaries of the past three weeks of lectures, using their class notes and memories. Although she thought she had delivered a seamless sequence of related ideas and examples, these summaries described disconnected topics, or "points." The students were getting most of the information down, but they were missing the frame of reference necessary for cohesive understanding of this material.

One of the best reasons for integrating writing with learning, therefore, is to give students time, reasons, and opportunities for understanding complex subjects: making connections among ideas and readings, grasping concepts they can use for further understanding, and thinking critically about the course material. Most teachers hope for these types of learning, but they will not occur if students are passively listening, reading, and taking notes primarily to absorb large amounts of information and to keep up with the rapid pace of your course.

In the political science class, for example, the written summaries of lectures revealed the way students were actually learning the subject. Other kinds of formal or informal writing could alter and enrich learning in the course:

(handwritten margin note: types of assignments I give)

- Leaving time for informal writing at the end of each class period, the teacher could explicitly ask students to explain connections between this lecture and previous classes or assigned readings.

- Writing about these connections, unresolved questions, or critical perspectives could be assigned outside class periods, possibly in response to focused study questions.

- Portions of class time could also be used for discussion of these questions, in pairs or small groups, linked with writing assignments.

(handwritten margin note: why discussions are heavy practice my classroom)

Writing and speaking can be used to construct particular kinds of understanding, and they also improve retention, because students are more likely to remember, as their own knowledge, what *they* have said than what teachers and texts have told them.

To a great extent, therefore, through carefully planned assignments and activities, you can create the kinds of learning experiences that correspond with your teaching goals. These forms of instruction will take time, in and outside class. Students will spend more time writing and speaking; you will spend less time speaking to them in class and will probably need to assign less reading. You won't be able to cover the amount of material you could include in a topical syllabus, designed for the continuous delivery of information. But for reasons we have explained, this kind of coverage is illusory. Covering less territory can improve the amount and the quality of learning in a course, if the course design offers students opportunities to process ideas and information and make knowledge of the subject their own.

As a schedule of topics, assignments, and other requirements for the term, a course syllabus cannot describe these learning activities in detail. When you begin to plan a course, it is most important to avoid composing a syllabus that *excludes* the kinds of learning you want students to experience. Rather than beginning with a series of topics and readings, therefore, begin by considering the kinds of learning you want to encourage. Integrated forms of student writing and class participation will correspond with these learning goals, in coordination with course material.

You can think of this approach to course design as a series of related questions:

- In what ways do I want students to learn this subject?

- What kinds of writing, reading, speaking, and listening will elicit these kinds of learning and requisite skills?

- What kinds of information do I need to provide — in lectures, assigned readings, instructions, and other course materials — to support these learning activities?

A course syllabus should follow from these questions. When you have answered them, you will know more realistically how to structure the use of class time each week and how much material you can reasonably cover without sacrificing the kinds of learning goals you want most to achieve.

Knowledge and Inquiry:
Two Models of Scholarship and Teaching

In our roles as college teachers we are also scholars: people who try to answer particular kinds of questions in our fields of study and who have (in the process of inquiry and in comparison with our students) acquired extensive knowledge. In teaching and in research, therefore, we can define our status in two related but different ways. We already know a great deal about our fields of study. To acquire and expand this knowledge, we pursue certain lines of inquiry. Both of these dimensions of scholarship can be used as a basis for teaching and course design, either separately or in combination. In other words:

1. We can view teaching as an opportunity to tell students what we know about a subject.

2. We can view teaching as an opportunity to engage students in the kinds of inquiry — and thus in the kinds of thinking and learning — we pursue.

The first of these models for scholarship and teaching encourages us to think of a course as a delivery system, and for reasons we have explained in previous sections of this chapter, this approach severely limits the kinds of language and learning skills students develop and use in a course. In advocating the model of inquiry, however, we do not suggest that lectures and other ways of delivering knowledge have no value in higher education. As Wilbert McKeachie observes in *Teaching Tips*, his classic guide for college teachers, lectures have specific functions of great potential value. Among them he notes the importance of delivering "up-to-date information on current research and theories," summarizing information that is widely dispersed in source material, adapting explanations to student audiences, illuminating implicit contradictions and issues, and conveying enthusiasm for the subject (69–72).

In any case, the lecture or "narration" is not just a type of course design. Periods of lecture can be usefully interspersed with discussion, writing activities, field or lab studies, and other kinds of learning. Even in a small, interactive seminar, sometimes we just need to explain things to students, and they just need to listen.

But these functions do not entirely explain the proportion of college teachers who design courses as delivery systems or the proportion of time they spend lecturing continuously, even to very small classes that could easily include and benefit from student participation. In other words, why do college teachers so often model their courses and teaching on the knowledge base they have established as scholars rather than on the kinds of inquiry they pursue? Why do they choose to tell students what they know rather than engage students in the kinds of questions they ask?

After all, most of us entered and have remained in our fields of study because there are so many interesting questions left unanswered, so many lines of inquiry still unexplored. Accumulated knowledge is satisfying in its own way, but the unsolved problems and unresolved debates are what make fields of research continually fascinating and creative. Knowledge and authority might constitute our stature, but investigation is what keeps us interested. Within these fields of inquiry we write to pursue and report on our investigations and to exchange views with people who have similar interests. These potential purposes for writing and learning engage students as well.

When they have finished teaching an undergraduate class, however, scholars who are most engaged in inquiry in their fields often ask "Are there any questions?" with the sense that if they have done a good job of teaching there won't be any questions left unanswered. Their students, in turn, feel that unanswered questions represent weakness or ignorance rather than occasions for further inquiry.

Here is the underlying pattern:

- While college teachers think of scholarship as inquiry or experimentation, they often think of teaching as conveying knowledge.

- And while scholars think of learning as exploration, discovery, and debate, they often lead their students to believe that learning is knowing: having the right information, ideas, and methods.

We can see the unfortunate effects of this pattern throughout the curriculum, in student writing and in other kinds of academic work. Unless they are explicitly encouraged to do so, undergraduates will not pursue questions and ideas that depart from the ones presented in lectures and readings. Teachers who assign and read informal student journals know that undergraduates do have these questions and make fascinating observations they could pursue in research and writing. When they are asked to write formal papers on the subject, however, the same students tend to take bland, predictable positions. In laboratory experiments, when undergraduates get unexpected results they assume that they did something wrong and that the experiment is ruined, like a fallen cake. They have been led to believe, as a colleague in chemistry complains, "that an experiment is the shortest distance between a known problem and a known solution."

The idea that learning represents knowledge, not inquiry, also explains why the roles of writing are so narrow in most undergraduate courses, even though writing is an essential medium of learning and exchange in all disciplines. If students believe that learning is knowing in a course, they will also believe that writing is not a medium of inquiry and exchange but a medium for demonstrating knowledge: a kind of take-home exam. If we do not deliberately revise this conception of learning, undergraduates will assume that every writing assignment requires the simulation of professorial knowledge, authority, and certainty that David Bartholomae describes in his essay "Inventing the University." Referring to his own field, Bartholomae argues that writing, in the undergraduate English class, "means having the knowledge of a professor of English" (140). Because students are taking other courses as well, they must write "as a literary critic one day and as an experimental psychologist the next" (135). And because they are not professional literary critics or experimental psychologists, assuming this knowledge means that as student writers they must continually "assume privilege without having any" (143).

This difficult but common rhetorical problem helps explain why undergraduate papers typically sound so stiff, cautious, formalized, and yet precarious, as though the writers were hanging on to the safest positions for dear life. As one student told us, "I felt that I'd mumbled a language that they [his teachers] speak fluently."

This is also why we recommend that for assigning and teaching writing in your discipline you should base your course design not on the body of content students should know but on the questions you want to raise, with plenty of occasions for students to raise questions of their own. Learning and writing, then, will become a process of looking for answers, examining sources of confusion, identifying further questions, and developing methods for solving problems. Such a course might begin, in fact, with the question *What is a good question in this field?*

We recognize that teaching a subject as a field of inquiry is easier in some fields and at some levels of instruction than in others, where new questions build upon an elaborate corpus of knowledge. Novels or historical documents might contain an enormous range of intriguing questions that undergraduates can explore in writing, even at the freshman level. In fields such as physics or biochemistry, students must spend most of their undergraduate studies assembling the basic knowledge from which questions emerge at the distant frontiers of graduate and professional research. Many of these fields use standard textbooks for instruction throughout the undergraduate curriculum. Real research in the social sciences involves field studies and other methods that undergraduates cannot easily use, due in part to necessarily stringent regulations on the use of human subjects.

But many teachers in the social sciences, sciences, and mathematics have developed investigative models for teaching undergraduates at all levels. These models do not question the need for basic factual and conceptual knowledge. They simply view the process of assembling knowledge as the main subject of a course. And almost all of these approaches use types of informal writing in the investigative process.

- In his numerous articles on learning styles, Richard Felder has advocated "multistyle approaches" to learning science and engineering. These include a wide range of problem-solving exercises that use writing.

- In his book *Experiencing Geometry*, David Henderson offers inductive methods for teaching principles of geometry throughout the mathematics curriculum. In Henderson's approach, writing is the central medium for following lines of inquiry in geometry.

- In their collection of essays *Writing to Learn Mathematics and Science*, Paul Connolly and Patricia Vilardi include a wide range of inductive, investigative strategies that place writing in the service of learning these subjects.

We know social scientists who have used publicly available data sets to construct writing assignments on data analysis and hypothesis formation, and others who ask their students both to write about and to follow guidelines on the use of human subjects in original social research.

There is another way in which you can think of teaching as inquiry or research, with or without asking undergraduates to do research in your field: You can think of teaching as research into the ways in which students actually learn the material. You can think of your course, therefore, as an ongoing experiment. To find out how this experiment is working, you will need data, and one of the most important functions of writing assignments is to give you information about the ways in which students grasp the concepts and information you consider most important. Student writing can chart otherwise unknown territory and provide points of reckoning on the map you need for steering a course, now and in following terms.

Writing, Reading, Speaking, and Listening for Active Learning

As an instrument of learning and inquiry, writing can take many forms, in conjunction with other uses of language. In a course that emphasizes active learning, these diverse forms of writing fall into place naturally, in lively interconnection with speaking, listening, and reading.

If you think of the class period as an occasion for stimulating thought and discussion, this shift in the function of the class opens many possibilities. "Preparing for class" is no longer just a matter of figuring out what you will say. Instead, you might consider the central issues you will raise and the ways in which you can best engage students in productive discussion of these issues, in writing and in speech. For example, you might speak for a few minutes to introduce central questions or problems you pose to the class and then give students five minutes or so to respond to the question in writing, as a basis for discussion. You can ask them to discuss issues in small groups that report back to the class or to come to class prepared for discussion, with written responses to readings or study questions.

These are just a few of the many possibilities for integrating writing activities with learning in courses of all sizes, in all fields of study. Teachers in the sciences and social sciences often assign collaborative research and writing projects — field studies, proposals, library projects, and lab experiments — that students complete in stages. These projects can provide occasions for valuable classroom activities, such as group presentations, poster sessions, and peer reviews of work in progress. Teachers in the humanities and social sciences often develop informal writing exercises that offer practice in close reading, analytical reading, and other important ways of approaching texts. They might also assign course journals or organize student-led discussions of readings, for which discussion leaders prepare written material. We describe these and many other strategies in Chapter 5, "Informal and Preparatory Writing," and Chapter 9, "Strategies for Including Writing in Large Courses."

You do not need to grade or even respond to all of this writing, though you will probably want to read it to find out what your students are thinking or to identify concepts that need further discussion. The types of informal writing we propose represent neglected but valuable functions of writing, overshadowed by the notion that all student work should be evaluated as a basis for grading. Informal exercises, linked with discussion, can be most valuable as preparations for the writing you do grade. Responses to study questions, brief summaries of readings, and notes on the substance of the class sessions also allow students to tell you, on a regular basis, what they understand, do not understand, or find most interesting. If these lively exchanges occur throughout the term, you will not need to wait for final evaluations to find out how well your course is working and how you can improve it.

New uses of writing will alter the roles of students more generally and will change the qualities of listening, reading, and speaking in the course. If students have responded to study questions, summarized readings, or submitted their own discussion questions in advance, they will come to class better prepared to contribute to discussions. In class, brief writing sessions in response to questions will have similar effects. If students know that you lecture for the purpose of providing background for periodic discussions, they will listen with a different quality of attention: not just to record what you are saying for the future purpose of taking an exam, but to assemble thoughts for a following exchange. Writing and listening will stimulate speaking. Reading, listening, and discussion will stimulate writing.

And students will think of themselves not just as passive recipients of knowledge, required periodically to demonstrate what they have learned; they will think of themselves as active participants in the class, partly responsible for its quality.

Safety First: Establishing Structure, Rules, and Standards

When they consider using innovative methods that integrate writing and learning, teachers often predict that their students will resist these departures from "normal" instruction in their disciplines, even in courses designated as writing-intensive or primarily geared toward writing instruction. And sometimes this prediction turns out to be correct. Students complain, complete assignments halfheartedly, ask "Why are we doing this?," or react to discussion questions with wary silence.

We recognize that when they enter a class students do bring with them certain expectations about teaching and learning, and these expectations vary from one discipline, institution, and group of students to another. Even in the same course students might be lively and adventurous one year and dull the next, due to changes in "chemistry" that are impossible to predict.

For these reasons we cannot promise that every strategy we recommend will work in your course, now or in future terms. But this is the nature of real experimentation, and the unpredictable factors are the ones that make teaching, like research, continually interesting. If a strategy doesn't work, or yields unexpected results, that's an opportunity to devise a modified approach. It doesn't mean the whole experiment should be thrown out and you should revert to the familiar, predictable methods you have always used.

Traditions of teaching in a discipline, related student expectations, and the chemistry of a class partly determine what will and will not work. But the chemistry of a particular group is itself a variable, not a constant. One factor that strongly influences these variations is a relative sense of safety.

Safety is a difficult factor to define, measure, or regulate, but it probably affects all social interaction. When we enter unfamiliar environments we assess, at some level, the extent to which we can safely relax and let down our guard. As long as a place seems potentially dangerous we remain, like other creatures, very cautious and easily startled.

Yet while the safety factor is hard to define, the basic principle for teaching is quite clear: If students feel safe in a class, they will participate in unfamiliar activities and even help to make these activities work; if students do not feel safe in a class, they will be reluctant even to speak.

From large amounts of anecdotal evidence we know that in the right circumstances, extremely shy students who are accustomed to formal instruction will participate comfortably in discussions, debates, presentations, and other activities. Yet in other circumstances a teacher might have difficulty getting the same students even to utter a sentence without feeling they were in danger. At the beginning of the term, in an advanced writing course, a student announced to one of us, with a look of stubborn terror, that she was simply too shy to participate in discussions, had never done so, and would not do so this semester, regardless of the consequences. Yet by the middle of the term she was participating in group activities, contributing to discussions, and reading her papers aloud to the class without hesitation. Asked how this change came about, she said she didn't know exactly. It just seemed natural for some reason, and safe.

How can we establish a sense of safety in a class?

Immediately breaking the ice with conversational activities can certainly help to reduce the tension in a room full of strangers. For example, asking students to interview and then introduce each other, in pairs, is a standard icebreaking method in small classes. In Chapter 8 we will suggest other methods for engaging students in open discussion and other activities.

While highly formal, structured relations between an authoritative teacher and submissive students can make students wary and silent, through fear of judgment, we want to emphasize that *a sense of safety does not result from the absence of structure, rules, and standards.*

student-centered
not teacher-passive

Perhaps the opposite is true. Especially if you want to depart from conventional methods and expectations, you need to do so very clearly. Students will go along with you in these activities if they know exactly what you are doing and why, and what the outcome of this activity will be. Clear rules, guidelines, and statements of purpose normalize the activity and establish a sense of safety, the more so if students receive these instructions in advance. That determinedly shy student would have been traumatized if we had suddenly asked her to stand before the class and read a paper, or discuss a reading. She began to participate, instead, in paired discussions of work in progress, with clear written questions she needed to address. She carried this kind of conversational participation to structured activities in larger groups, and then to discussions with the entire class.

> The most lively, productive interaction in classes usually results from clearly structured guidelines. Unstructured classes and undirected activities can in fact seem the most hazardous to students, because from one moment to the next they do not know what is going to happen to them.

precisely

If you ask students to discuss drafts of their papers in small groups without detailed procedures they can follow, for example, they will spend most of the allotted time awkwardly figuring out how to proceed. We recommend giving them a sheet that lists procedures for work in groups, including the specific features of the drafts they should discuss and the amount of time they should spend on each one. If you ask students to do informal writing in class, they should know why they are writing and what the outcome of this work will be. *Who will read it? For what purpose? Will you grade this writing?* If they don't know the answers to these questions in advance, they won't know what they are doing.

A sense of safety results less from the kinds of activities in a class than from the students' trust in you and in the behavior of other students in these activities. This trust is not just a warm, fuzzy sense of well-being. It results from confidence that you will establish and maintain rules that protect them from humiliation, conflict, and unnecessary confusion. If they have this confidence and a clear sense of what they are doing, students will participate freely in unfamiliar learning activities.

Designing Writing Assignments and Assignment Sequences

Key Elements

Think of Assignments as *Your* Writing for the Course   30

Essay assignments constitute one of the two most important kinds of writing we do for our students: the other is our written responses to their essays (the subject of the next chapter).

The Rhetoric of Assignment Writing: Subject, Audience, Purpose, and Form   31

Teaching writing can be a kind of research on the ways in which students learn the subject of your course. From this perspective, you can also think of writing assignments as research instruments: tools for finding out what students know, think, and believe on a given subject. To write effective assignments, therefore, you must take some basic rhetorical factors into account: the subject of a question, its purpose, the form of the response, and who the respondents are.

Designing Assignments with Rhetorical Clarity   33

For each assignment, the student should be able to answer these questions:

- What am I, the author, writing about?
- For whom?
- For what purpose?
- In what form?

Consider these rhetorical conditions for student writing:

- The primary conditions for student writing: you and your course.
- Imaginary or hypothetical conditions for student writing.
- Real audiences and purposes as conditions for student writing.

Defining Boundaries Clearly 38

Regardless of their rhetorical conditions, good assignments clearly define the boundaries within which students are free to write.

Sequencing Writing Assignments to Build a Course of Study 40

If you integrate writing with learning in your course design, writing assignments will not be isolated, disconnected occasions for writing practice; they will constitute a sequence that contributes to the overall shape and purpose of your course. What principles might govern an assignment sequence?

- *Move from simple to complex tasks.*
- *Consider the order of writing activities in your field.*
- *Precede the theoretical/abstract with the experiential/concrete.*
- *Sequence assignments to build a frame of reference.*
- *Use repetition to measure progress.*

Thinking of Assignments (and Courses) as Progressions 46

Thoughtfully designed and arranged in sequence, writing assignments have enormous potential to support directed movement through the learning process, as integral components of a course of study.

Think of Assignments as *Your* Writing for the Course

Essay assignments constitute one of the two most important kinds of writing we do for our students. The other is our written responses to their essays. Nevertheless, we often put far too little time into planning assignments and neglect to consider that what we write can dramatically affect how well our students will write in return. Whether we use assignments to help our students understand the material of a course, to evaluate their understanding, or to teach specific skills, assignments are the springboards that propel our students into action. What they do next will depend upon what we say.

Ironically, instructors often get into trouble with writing assignments because they do not think of them as writing, let alone as important writing. While preparing these assignments, we don't follow the advice we give our students: draft, revise, get someone else to read the text, and revise again. Instead, we tend to design assignments haphazardly. We may not write them out at all, relying on informal instructions given verbally at the end of class rather than giving students a carefully formulated text they can refer to. Teachers often write all of the course assignments quickly when they are composing a syllabus, without revising them when the term is under way, or invent each assignment as the need arises, shortly before class. We also tend to reproduce the kinds of assignments we had to complete as students, without recalling how tedious or confusing they might have been or why the good ones worked in contexts different from those of our classes.

When teachers produce an assignment quickly, without considering its strategic functions in the course, they rarely explain the purpose of the assignment to their students, often because they have not considered its purpose themselves. And if they do not think of the assignment as a piece of written communication they composed, they often blame their students for inconsistent and disappointing results.

The Rhetoric of Assignment Writing: Subject, Audience, Purpose, and Form

We proposed in Chapter 1 that you can profitably think of teaching writing as a kind of research on the ways in which students learn the subject of your course. From this perspective, you can also think of writing assignments as research instruments: tools for finding out what students know, think, and believe on a given subject. A questionnaire, like a writing assignment, is itself a form of writing, and social scientists know that even minor differences in the phrasing of a question can elicit very different answers from the same respondents. Ambiguous questions will yield ambiguous or inconsistent replies. Unfamiliar terms and concepts, or confusing instructions, will make a questionnaire difficult to complete and reduce the quality and proportion of returns. If people don't understand why you asked a question, their answers will become wary and unreliable. Yet a good question should elicit an interesting range of comparable responses. Social research instruments work best when the respondents can easily understand the language and purposes of the questions and when those questions make enough sense in the context of their own experience to elicit genuine, thoughtful replies.

To write an effective questionnaire, therefore, social scientists have to take some basic rhetorical factors into account. They need to make clear

- the *subject of a question*,
- its *purpose*, and
- the *form of the response*.

To do this they need to consider

- *who the respondents are* and
- *what they are likely to understand.*

Yet scholars who put this thought and care into their research often simply tell students to do something, without considering whether the terms, purpose, and form of the assignment are clear to its intended audience. In composing writing assignments, as in their other research, teachers also need to take rhetorical factors into account.

Example of Rhetorical Context

In an interdisciplinary teaching workshop, a historian passed around a draft of a writing assignment that presented a quotation from an assigned text and said, simply, "Discuss, in four pages."

In a tone of deep suspicion, a biologist in the group asked, "What does *discuss* mean, exactly?"

The historian thought for a moment and said, "Well, I guess it means 'Make an argument about what the quotation means.'" As he said this he had already realized that he needed to clarify the term *discuss* for his students, who were not necessarily history majors, and the discussion then turned to the meaning of the word *argument*.

For this historian, "make an argument" had a specific, complex meaning, on the order of "From your own perspective, situate this quotation in the context of the course, in relation to other interpretations of the same events." But this conception of an argument differed from the kinds of arguments teachers might expect in political science, sociology, biology, or literary studies. While an argument in political science, for example, might be stated very directly as a thesis at the beginning of a paper and then supported by formal presentation of evidence and reasoning, historical arguments are often more subtly embedded in the way the writer narrates events and uses primary sources.

How could students in a history course make such complex inferences from the word *discuss*? A few of the most experienced history majors might understand what this teacher wanted them to do. The most bold or hopelessly confused students might ask for clarification. Other capable, responsible students might misinterpret the assignment and complete the wrong kind of paper. Like a faulty research instrument, such an assignment primarily tests the students' abilities to figure out what the assignment really means, through trial and error. While "psyching out what the teacher really wants" may be a useful skill for undergraduates, it is probably not your main goal for an assignment or a very fair basis for evaluation.

In the following sections we cannot describe all of the specific features and functions that might help to make particular types of assignments clear to students. Even in the case of arguments, there are too many variations among disciplines, levels of instruction, and specific course goals. Instead, we will explore the implications of this example in ways that encourage you to develop assignments that work, like good research questions, according to the goals of your own courses and disciplines.

Designing Assignments with Rhetorical Clarity

Because assignments are types of writing that elicit other types of writing, the rhetorical clarity you build into an assignment should help establish similar clarity for student writers.

On the basis of your assignment, students should be able to answer some basic questions about the subject, audience, purpose, and form of their work:

- What am I, the author, writing about?
- For whom?
- For what purpose?
- In what form?

If an assignment is clear, your students should know the answers to these questions — from the assignment itself or from the context of your course — as they begin to work on the project. Clarifying these questions is especially important in undergraduate courses because the rhetorical features of student writing, compared with other kinds of written communication, can be rather murky. If you are writing an article for a particular journal, for example, you can answer these four questions quite easily. You have specific things you want to say about a topic, for readers of that journal, for reasons grounded in your career and discipline. The form and style of articles in that journal are either familiar to you or easy to determine by looking at back issues and guidelines for submissions. The rhetorical conditions for writing might be difficult, but they are not, as a rule, ambiguous.

The Primary Conditions for Student Writing: You and Your Course

By contrast, undergraduates typically write about subjects that are new to them, in forms that are unfamiliar. They also write primarily for their teachers, for the purpose of completing assignments and learning what they did not previously know. These are what we will call the *primary* conditions for student writing. Although we will describe further conditions for student writing — other audiences and purposes — these primary conditions always apply when we assign and evaluate writing in our courses.

Because our students are writing primarily to meet our expectations in the contexts of our classes, we are responsible for making those expectations as clear as possible.

- To what extent should we define the topic of the paper?

- What standards will we, as the primary audience, use to evaluate this work?

- What is the purpose of this assignment, in the context of the course?

- What form should the writing take?

We often presume that figuring out the answers to these questions is the writer's responsibility and that students will just know, somehow, what we want them to do. But ambiguous assignments create unnecessary frustration and confusion, and the resulting papers often represent lucky or unlucky guesswork, not the levels of knowledge, effort, and skill we want to assess.

For example, many assignments just pose a question, without any rhetorical context.

> What is Steven Pinker's central argument in *How the Mind Works,* and who is he arguing against?

Most students will read this assignment essentially as an exam question and task of identification. They will assume that you have a particular Right Answer in mind and will devote much of their thought to figuring out what you want them to say. If you want instead for them to develop and explain their own interpretations, you need to make that expectation clear, as in the following examples. The first is a revised version of the cognitive psychology assignment on Stephen Pinker's work.

Sample Assignments

In four pages, explain what you consider to be the most important argument in Steven Pinker's *How the Mind Works,* with examples and quotations that support your interpretation. There are several themes you might reasonably choose to emphasize. I want to know which one you consider the most important, and how well you can make your case.

Matthew Evangelista, a professor in government, made his expectations even more explicit in this assignment for a first-year writing seminar:

Assignment: Our in-class debate focused on the policy of the United States toward its NATO ally Turkey in light of that country's treatment of its ethnic Kurds. For this assignment, write the first draft of a short essay arguing against the position your side adopted in the debate. Bring the draft with you to class this Thursday, where a member of the opposing side will work with you on editing and revising it. *Purpose:* This assignment is intended to help develop your skills in relating evidence to argument and considering counterarguments and evidence that does not support your own position. The peer-editing process should also enhance your skills in editing and revising.

For an upper-level seminar, Evangelista asked this question:

In order to sort out the most important factors and explanations for a particular phenomenon, political scientists sometimes employ "counterfactual history." To take a simple example, one might argue that if Roosevelt had lived longer or Stalin had died sooner, the cold war would never have happened. Try to find from among the readings an explicit or implicit counterfactual argument and analyze it. Consider, for example, the assumptions it makes about the most important level of analysis (in the case above, it would be the individual level — the "great person theory of history") and about the most important explanations for the cold war. The goal of the paper is to think critically about alternative courses that postwar Soviet-American relations might have taken as a way to understand the main factors that influenced the cold war.

The differences between these assignments reflect Evangelista's awareness of what he can reasonably expect students to do at different levels of study in his field: who his students are, what they already know, what they are likely to understand, and the kind of assignment they will be able to complete. Yet at both levels he clearly defines the subject, purpose, and form of the writing he wants students to produce.

Imaginary or Hypothetical Conditions for Student Writing

In addition to these primary conditions for student writing, for you and your courses, there are often hypothetical conditions that can make assignments more explicit, meaningful, and interesting. Because you create these occasions for writing, you are free to modify and specify the rhetorical conditions you want students to imagine as they write. In fact, most assignments have implicitly imaginary, hypothetical features. When you assign a "paper" or an "essay" in your course, you are actually looking, perhaps, for a particular kind of argument, analysis, explanation, or report, rooted in your discipline. As David Bartholomae observes, you are asking students to write *as though* they were professional literary scholars, historians, political scientists, or developmental psychologists: to approximate that kind of knowledge and authority, that kind of position and perspective.

Remember that if you have a particular form of writing in mind, you should explain what that form is, or show students examples. You can't reasonably expect them to invent forms you haven't described.

You can also ask students explicitly to pretend that they are other kinds of writers, writing for imaginary audiences, in forms appropriate for those imagined contexts.

We know teachers who have asked their students to imagine that they were writing articles for particular periodicals, such as *Scientific American* or *Psychology Today*, or letters on specific issues to the editors of particular newspapers. Other teachers have asked students to imagine that they were political or scientific advisers to presidents or senators or that they were consultants assigned to recommend, in the form of a memo or a report, reorganization strategies for a particular corporation. Undergraduates usually enjoy this explicitly playful adoption of personae, and because imitation is a natural, powerful way to learn language, they are surprisingly good at adopting imaginary voices and styles.

Sample Assignment

In his course on the history and literature of Islamic Spain, Ross Brann gave his students a choice between two similar assignments. One assumed primary rhetorical conditions, asking them to describe a type of historical figure, in a conventional academic essay. The other applied hypothetical rhetorical conditions, asking them to imagine that they *were* that figure, writing in a form and style characteristic of the period:

1. Draw a portrait of an Andalusian *adib* (literary intellectual). What must such a person know and how must he behave? Describe how this *adib* served Andalusian courtly society, what his life was like, his view of the world, what kinds of poetry he preferred and wrote, and why he preferred them.

2. Imagine that you are an Andalusian *adib* living in tenth-century Córdoba. Write a letter to a like-minded friend in North Africa (or Barcelona) and describe your life so as to convince him to join you at the Umayyad court. Also tell him something about your favorite genre of poetry and what you have been hearing and writing lately.

The great majority of Brann's students chose the second option and wrote with remarkably lively historical and literary imagination. Adopting this unlikely persona seemed more interesting and enjoyable to them, if not easier, than pretending they were academic authorities on Islamic Spain.

Real Audiences and Purposes as Conditions for Student Writing

We should also recognize that student writing does not have to be a hypothetical exercise, performed exclusively for teachers to demonstrate the potential to communicate with others. Students can actually write for other audiences, including one another, for purposes that extend beyond the completion of course requirements.

From his interviews with Harvard seniors (summarized in the book *Making the Most of College: Students Speak Their Minds*), Richard Light identified three major factors that made writing and writing instruction most effective for these students:

- "They believe they learn most effectively when writing instruction is organized around a substantive discipline" rather than used to teach abstract, general skills (59).

- They learned most from teachers who invited and respected diverse interpretations and were most frustrated when "the teacher seems to forget whose paper it is, and begins to change the voice of an essay from the student's voice to the teacher's voice" (60).

- "Students identify the courses that had the most profound impact on them as courses in which they wrote papers, not just for the professor, as usual, but for their fellow students as well" (64).

The first observation supports our recommendation in the previous chapter that writing should be integrated as much as possible with learning in the course and discipline. The second recommends assignments and responses that explicitly encourage independent thinking and motivation for writing. The third point suggests that assignments and the broader contexts of the course should create real occasions for students to read and respond to one another's work. In the following chapters we will suggest a variety of methods for organizing this exchange and making students real audiences for student writing.

Readers beyond the classroom can also become real, primary audiences, for purposes important to larger communities. Letters to the editors of newspapers can be sent and are sometimes published. Letters to political and community leaders and agencies can also be sent to those intended readers, and so can some kinds of research papers and reports of relevance to particular organizations.

Sample Assignment

In his writing-intensive section of an evolutionary biology course, Cornell graduate student Brian Traw gave the following assignment:

> Write a letter to the Kansas Board of Education in favor of the reinstatement of evolution as a topic that should be covered in high

school biology. At least part of your letter should be devoted to the question of what is fact versus theory with respect to evolution.

At the time, the fall of 1999, this was an important national issue in science education, and along with other background information and discussion, Traw's assignment included a copy of a *New York Times* article, "Board for Kansas Deletes Evolution from Curriculum." This assignment allowed biology majors to participate directly in a national debate of great relevance to education in their field.

Defining Boundaries Clearly

Regardless of the rhetorical conditions you build into them, good assignments clearly define the boundaries within which students are free to write. This premise acknowledges that if writing is to be anything more than copying or following instructions, writers must have some freedom to take positions, develop ideas, and choose language that communicates what they have to say. However, freedom becomes meaningful and constructive only within boundaries, and unclear boundaries — even very broad ones — tend to restrict freedom by making every move seem potentially a wrong move.

Clear boundaries for writing can be very broadly or narrowly focused, loosely or tightly structured, with lots of room or very little room for choices. You might give students freedom to write about any theme that interests them in an assigned reading, or you might ask them to answer a very specific question about a single quotation. We've found that students are about evenly divided in their preferences for open or tightly structured assignments, so you won't be able to please everyone unless you offer a choice of assignment types. Whether they like the scope of the assignment or not, however, students should know clearly where your role as the teacher ends and where their roles, choices, and responsibilities as writers begin.

Counterproductive Clarifications

Lack of clarity sometimes results from omission, but teachers often obscure the boundaries of an assignment by offering suggestions, hints, examples, and "clarifications" that imply a hidden agenda and thus qualify the freedom they have previously defined. When they have defined the general boundaries of the assignment, teachers often qualify these boundaries with signal phrases such as the following:

You might want to consider. . . .

For example, on page 25 Bloom states. . . .

While you are writing, you might want to keep the following questions in mind:

When you are tempted to add "clarifications" to an assignment, you might keep the following warnings in mind:

- When you find yourself adding helpful suggestions, remember that students will almost invariably read might to mean should.
- Students will also tend (despite your injunctions to the contrary) to interpret examples as prescriptions: indications of what you really want them to do but aren't saying outright.
- If you include lists of examples, questions, or points they "might" find useful, student writers will also tend to use these sequences as organizational guidelines. When you read their papers, you will find that suggestions you listed at random, as they happened to occur to you, will appear in the same order, as though you had prescribed a logical sequence for writing and thinking about the topic.

The truth of the matter, in most cases, is that we continue to think about the boundaries of the assignment while we are writing it, and those qualifications represent second, further thoughts as we begin to envision the kind of paper we hope students will produce. So we add those further thoughts in a casual, offhand manner that students will not take casually at all — and for good reason. These apparently random suggestions often do offer clues to the real expectations with which we will read papers, even if we haven't fully realized those expectations ourselves.

The solution to this problem is either to stop yourself when you begin to offer "hints" or to revise the assignment in ways that build these hints into redefined boundaries. If you make the first decision, when you read the papers you must honor the freedom you have given students and not hold them accountable for unstated expectations. If you take the second option, you should state very clearly the questions you want students to consider or the approach they should take as guidelines for writing.

Examples

In the Kansas Board of Education assignment (see p. 37), Brian Traw would have made his instructions more ambiguous if he had said, "In your letter you might want to consider the question of what is fact versus theory with respect to evolution." He could have clarified and broadened the students' range of choices by deleting this specific suggestion. Deciding that it was an essential part of his own expectations, he said, "a part of your letter should be devoted to the questions of what is fact versus theory." In doing so, he both narrowed and clarified the boundaries in which his students were free to write.

If these narrower boundaries include lists and other sequences (for instance, if you add two or three other directives to the one already included for the evolution essay), remember that most students will use these sequences as models for organization. As a consequence, you need to present them in a logical order that could be used as a model for organization. Recall Ross Brann's first essay topic (the one few students chose):

> Draw a portrait of an Andalusian *adib* (literary intellectual). What must such a person know and how must he behave? Describe how this *adib* served Andalusian courtly society, what his life was like, his view of the world, what kinds of poetry he preferred and wrote, and why he preferred them.

Students who choose this topic will probably take up each of the points Brann suggests in the order in which he suggests them. They will begin with knowledge and behavior, turn to roles and functions at the court, describe the *adib*'s lifestyle, add a section on his view of the world, and so on. Does this sequence represent a logical progression and a good template for organization? If they follow this list, student writers will treat its items as separate points of equal importance, whereas tastes in poetry and roles in courtly society are not separate from knowledge, behavior, and way of life.

Sequencing Writing Assignments to Build a Course of Study

Thus far we've discussed the qualities and functions of individual writing assignments. If you integrate writing with learning in your course design, however, these assignments will not be isolated, disconnected occasions for writing practice; they will constitute a sequence that contributes to the overall shape and purpose of your course. Like writing itself, courses usually have a narrative quality of movement that carries students from one level of knowledge and understanding to another. If you think of the beginning of your course as a point of departure in this learning process, assignment sequences should help carry students through this process toward a particular destination.

The revision of course designs, in turn, includes the revision of assignments and sequences to create a more effective progression. When individual writing assignments do not work, the reason is not necessarily that they are bad assignments. Teachers often realize instead that an assignment worked poorly because it called for knowledge and skills the students did not yet possess or was in other ways misplaced in the sequence.

What principles should govern this developmental sequence? Particular subjects, levels, teaching goals, and disciplines affect sequences so heavily that the specific answers to this question are almost as numerous as listings in the course catalog. But there are some general principles you can probably apply to your course, if you identify the progression of learning goals in the course and then consider the ways in which specific types of writing correlate with those goals.

Sequencing Assignments: Moving from Simple to Complex Tasks

This would seem to be an obvious principle, but we have observed many course plans that immediately ask students to write the kinds of papers they might be able to complete well only at the end of the term, such as complex analyses or comparisons of very difficult, theoretical texts. Asking a student who has read only one text in a field to critique its strengths and weaknesses may be asking for the impossible. When students can't meet these high expectations, teachers often have to revise their plans with a sense of disappointment that undermines morale.

WHAT MAKES AN ASSIGNMENT SIMPLE? There are a number of features other than brevity that can make assignments relatively simple in a sequence:

- Writing short papers before writing longer ones.
- Writing about one reading selection before comparing or synthesizing two or more readings.
- Explaining a basic concept before applying that concept to new problems or cases.
- Summarizing a text before analyzing, interpreting, or criticizing a text.
- Explaining one author's argument before developing one's own argument on the issue.

We will amplify these and other bases for sequences in following sections.

Sequencing Assignments: Consider the Order of Writing Activities in Your Field

To begin a sequence with a relatively simple assignment, you do not need to start beneath the level of serious work in your course. In most fields of study, simple writing tasks are embedded in complex ones, within the whole process of assembling and communicating knowledge, and these embedded forms often constitute a developmental sequence.

WRITING SUMMARIES In fields in which students usually write about texts, the task of summarizing a text is not just a separate, rudimentary form of writing and is not necessarily easy. Summary is an essential part of interpretation, comparison, critical analysis, and other complex kinds of writing. In fact, many flawed arguments and interpretations result from misunderstanding or misrepresentation of what the author actually said. Critical essays often begin with a clear summary to convince readers that the criticism is fair.

Summaries themselves can take different forms, used to cultivate particular skills:

- Sequential gloss or "plot summary"
- An account of the author's central argument and evidence
- Identification of the underlying assumptions used to build an argument
- Description of the structure or organization of the text

WORKING WITH BASIC TERMS AND CONCEPTS   Some fields in the humanities — such as film, theater, and the history of art — require knowledge of basic terms and concepts used in interpretive and critical writing. It makes sense to design early assignments that develop mastery of these linguistic and conceptual foundations.

Sample Assignments

Lynda Bogel, who teaches first-year writing seminars on the study of film, finds it useful in one of her first essay assignments to give students a well-defined, simple task that calls on their study of specifics (such as props, symbols, lighting) and modes of interpretation. She asks them to choose an assertion to refute, giving consideration to counterarguments. For example, students might tackle this assertion about the film *Thelma and Louise*:

> There's a lot of pointless, filler scenery in *Thelma and Louise* — endless vistas, vast expanses of open deserts and canyons, unpopulated blue skies, secondary roads stuffed with horns, oil derricks, sirens, Mack trucks (you even get trucks filled with blue skies). In a film about a growing friendship between two women on the run, all these settings seem a meaningless way to extend the film's length.

In another early, fairly simple assignment, Bogel asks students to apply basic terms and concepts in film studies to the analysis of a single scene:

> Choose one of the following scenes from Psycho to analyze in detail, considering the way the various aspects of the scene (cinematography, mise-en-scène, editing, soundtrack, etc.) contribute to its overall effect.
> The real estate office scene
> Marion driving her cars
> The shower sequence (including Norman "cleaning up")
> Lila exploring the Bates house
> The psychiatrist's "explanation"

OBSERVATION AND DESCRIPTION   In courses that involve field studies or laboratory research, observation and description naturally precede, and then become part of, the presentation and analysis of data in full reports. Rather than assigning full reports first, many teachers initially focus on field and lab notes, then on the development of hypotheses and methods, before asking students to write introductions, discussion sections, and abstracts. Full reports or research proposals therefore emerge from the kinds of writing and thinking that, in professional studies, lead to them. As we will observe in Chapter 7, library research papers also result from a series of writing and reading activities that can be usefully assigned in sequence.

For these reasons, you might think of "simple" assignments as "prior tasks."

Sequencing Assignments: Precede the Theoretical/Abstract with the Experiential/Concrete

As a rule, students have considerable difficulty grasping theories, abstract concepts, and associated readings without prior attention to cases, concrete examples, or connection with personal experience. Many of the "prior tasks" we have mentioned, such as field and laboratory notes, are also forms of writing based on direct experience and hands-on learning.

In science classes, students can usually grasp general, abstract concepts more easily if they first attempt to explain concrete examples. In an anthropology course on the ritual process, students might begin by describing specific rituals from their own experience, such as weddings or fraternity initiations, before they read descriptions and theoretical accounts of rituals in other cultures. A course on the history or political theory of women's work might initially ask students to outline work histories of women in their families over three generations and then describe the changes they observe over time. In the social sciences, students can better understand theories if they first examine detailed cases that situate theoretical positions in people's lives. Literature courses often begin by asking students to connect events and themes in a work of literature with dimensions of their own experience.

Sample Assignment

In a first-year writing seminar on women and space, Antonia Losano, at the time a graduate student in English at Cornell, used a series of short essays to prepare her students for a longer, more abstract discussion of gender and space in Virginia Woolf's *A Room of One's Own*. In an opening essay students wrote a description of a special space at Cornell that they had explored for this purpose; another essay then asked them to theorize, as a sociologist, feminist, or cultural critic, their experience of one day's activities at Cornell. Several increasingly complex assignments followed. By the time students wrote on Woolf, they were well prepared to take a sophisticated approach.

*Sequencing Assignments: Sequence Assignments
to Build a Frame of Reference*

It's at least daunting, if not unreasonable, to ask students to write as
though they were authorities when they are not — to take positions on
an issue, for example, when they have no basis for forming a position.
The problem is aggravated by the fact that American students, especially, are often accustomed to making flimsy arguments — pulled out
of a hat as "personal opinion" — on complex issues they know little
about. In their secondary schools, most undergraduates were asked to
take positions on issues such as capital punishment and abortion in
short essays, with little reference to the vast arenas of national debate.
If you assign such arguments prematurely, therefore, the problem is
that your students *will* complete the assignments as opinion pieces.
And you will have to figure out what to do next. If one of your goals is to
teach your students how to develop a substantial argument, it makes
sense for you to delay this kind of assignment — even to prohibit students from taking a position — until they have a solid basis for developing and supporting one with explicit assumptions, sufficient evidence,
and acknowledgment of differing views.

Sample Assignments

For the purpose of delaying students' taking a position, you can use
earlier assignments to build the frame of reference from which positions
emerge and become meaningful. Summaries and comparisons of
central arguments in assigned readings, annotated bibliographies, and
library research exercises can be useful ways to build this frame of
reference.

You can also begin by asking students to adopt the viewpoints —
or even the voices — of authors they read. Like many other teachers,
sociologist Michael Macy has recognized that his students have
difficulty applying theories to cases with critical awareness of the
degree of "fit" between them. Students have this difficulty in part
because they do not have a point of view from which they can recognize the usefulness and limitations of theory. To help them establish this
position in his course Group Solidarity, Macy asks students to analyze
a specific case initially from the viewpoint of a particular theorist and
then from the viewpoint of another theorist, so they can register the
effects of differing perspectives. When they have grasped what it
means to have a well-defined theoretical position for analyzing cases,
he asks them in the culminating assignment to test the predictions of a
single theory with reference to two related case studies. They cannot do
this, Macy has found, until they realize from earlier assignments that
social theories offer ways of understanding cases from particular
positions — points of view — juxtaposed to others.

Macy observes, "If students analyze only one case, they tend simply to use the case to illustrate the theory, selectively noting elements of the case that illustrate the corresponding theoretical ideas. When I require them to compare cases, . . . they have to consider whether the differences in the cases can be accounted for by the theory. I have found that a comparative perspective fundamentally changes the way students write, moving them from descriptive to analytical accounts."

If Macy had made his final assignment at the beginning of the term, without prior assignments that build a frame of reference, the learning process would have been inverted: he would have spent the following weeks trying to explain to his students what they did wrong and what they should have done instead.

Sequencing Assignments: Use Repetition to Measure Progress

While recommending that you move from simple to complex, or from concrete to abstract, we recognize the potential value of repeating types of assignments or even repeating the same assignment at different times in the term.

There are very few skills that one can master in one attempt. Michael Macy's sociology students needed to complete more than one analysis of a case, from more than one perspective, to register the importance and effects of differing theoretical positions. Antonia Losano's students experimented in a variety of ways with space and theories before writing their final essays on Woolf.

Sample Assignments

Brief assignments such as study questions or one-page summaries of readings can provide weekly practice in a consistent form even as major assignments change. Because some kinds of writing are embedded in others, however, you can also build certain amounts of repetition and practice into a progression of writing tasks. If you start with the writing of summaries, you can ask students to begin critical, analytical, and comparative papers with summaries of the arguments they address in each paper. This explicit guideline will make students aware that they are continuing to practice and develop skills used at the beginning of the term.

To help students recognize what they have learned, teachers also repeat early assignments at the end of the term. At the end of a course, teachers of film studies sometimes ask students to repeat the assignment on the first film they watched. This repetition allows them to measure changes in the ways they watch, analyze, and write about films in general. If you begin your course by asking students to write on the basis of personal experience, as in the student descriptions of ritual, it can be useful to have them describe the same experiences at the end of the term, with knowledge and perspectives they gained in the intervening weeks.

Thinking of Assignments (and Courses) as Progressions

Our discussion of assignments and sequences in this chapter suggests some correlations between good courses and good writing, both of which embody principles of structure and of movement.

In both cases these qualities of structure and movement are interdependent but represent different kinds of order, one categorical and the other sequential. In other words, we can think of a course or an essay categorically as a topic broken into subtopics, as in a conventional syllabus or outline. We can also think of a course or an essay as a progression: a connected series of ideas and information that moves us from one position or level of understanding to another.

The term *course* itself (as used in navigation) suggests this quality of movement in a direction, from one place to another, and the root meanings of *essay* — to try out or test something (in Latin and French) — suggest exploration and experimentation.

We have emphasized consideration of sequence, progression, and connection not because topical structure is unimportant, but because the means of progression tend more to be neglected. When teachers plan courses, as we noted in Chapter 1, they usually begin with decisions about the range of topics they will cover, and while they arrange these topics in a logical sequence, their plans do not always extend to ways of moving students through a process of learning. As a representation of topical structure, a course syllabus usually looks skeletal, without the life and flesh necessary for movement.

When teachers continue to think of their courses as topical structures, they also tend to think of writing assignments in relation to topics covered at particular times: "This week students will write about Topic A; next week we will turn to Topic B." This correlation of assignments with course topics is obviously necessary, but it does not take into account the process through which students develop knowledge and skills as learners of this material and as writers in a discipline.

Thoughtfully designed and arranged in sequence, writing assignments have enormous potential to support directed movement through the learning process, as integral components of a course of study.

3

What Can You Do with Student Writing?

Key Elements

The Silent Transaction   48

In preparation for reading, responding to, and evaluating student writing, pause to consider what you are about to do and why, along with some potential alternatives.

An Approach to Avoid: Reading Student Writing with Grading as a Goal   49

The proper place for grading is at the end of the process of reading and responding to student papers, not at the beginning. The process should begin with reading. Be wary of becoming one of three types of graders: the grading machine, the instructive grader, the copy editor.

What Students Prefer   53

Students value thoughtful feedback that engages them in dialogue with their teachers. They see this feedback as an essential part of the writing process and as a foundation for their development. You cannot expect good writing to matter to them if it does not appear to count in your approach to response.

A Basic Method for Responding to Student Writing 55

1. Read through each paper receptively, letting it communicate whatever it is trying to say.
2. Compose a reply to the writer as a set of organized comments at the end of the paper, on the back, or on a separate page.
3. When you have written the final comments, go back into the student's text and insert specific questions, suggestions, or praise.
4. Then, if necessary, determine the grade.

Using (and Saving) Time Wisely 58

You can adapt the method for responding to student writing to a wide range of circumstances and course sizes if you keep some basic principles and techniques in mind:

- Give reading essays priority over grading them.
- Avoid line editing and random, reactive comments.
- Respond to key issues you have identified and emphasized in advance as important.
- Respond to the writer as a reader, in final comments that emphasize the most important features of the paper.
- When you return to the text, limit yourself to comments you can be reasonably sure the writer will understand and put to use.

Further Suggestions for Adapting Strategies to Your Own Circumstances and Inclinations 59

Breaking the Silence: The Student's Role in Response 60

Ask students what they think of their work before they turn it in. In class, students can write a note to you on the backs of their papers about strengths, weaknesses, and areas for improvement.

Variations on This Exercise 61

The Silent Transaction

The question of what you should do with student papers arises at a particular moment in the conventional process of assigning and evaluating student writing. You have given students an assignment due in a particular class period; your students have (you hope) completed this assignment by the deadline. And during that class, or at the end, you say, "Please turn in your papers."

Freshly completed, unmarked papers then sail quietly across the sea between students and teacher like new little ships, into your hands. What will happen to them next is up to you.

In later sections of this chapter we will suggest ways in which you can interrupt and alter this silent transaction. Initially, however, we'll assume that you will next do what students are fully conditioned to expect: take these papers home or to your office, where you will eventually read, evaluate, and mark them. And when you have finished this task, in another class period these little ships will sail back in various conditions to their owners, who will find out how well their writing weathered the journey.

Even if you perform your expected role in this exchange, you have a number of options. After you receive student papers, in other words, there are several possible answers to the question *What should I do with them?* Before you begin to do whatever seems the normal, natural, or right thing to do, without thinking, it can be useful to pause to consider what you are about to do and why, along with some potential alternatives.

An Approach to Avoid: Reading Student Writing with Grading as a Goal

If we found you at work on a pile of student papers and asked, *What are you doing?* most of you would say you were *grading* these papers. Of course *grading* covers the whole process of reading, writing comments, and evaluating papers, but it is not just a random figure of speech. Teachers say they are *grading* papers because the ultimate necessity of assigning grades tends to assert a cognitive priority over the entire task, from beginning to end. Grading becomes the aim of the exercise.

After all, you would not say you were *grading* other written material you read: professional articles, novels, letters from friends, or even drafts that colleagues ask you to review. When we approach writing receptively, as a form of communication, we usually say we are *reading*. And if that communication is part of a dialogue — an exchange — we then *reply* or *comment*. *Grading* is a kind of reading and response we reserve almost exclusively for student writing.

Grades assume this control over our approaches to student work because they are the main forms of currency in undergraduate education and the most powerful symbols of achievement. At the end of the term and for most course projects, grading is a necessity, not an option. For this reason there is no point in arguing that grading systems should be abolished or that we should pretend grades are unimportant. Instead, we need to consider the ways in which the institutional importance of grades tends to define student writing — for teachers and for students — as an object of evaluation, not as a form of communication.

While we can't deny this importance, we can reduce its negative effects by putting grading in its appropriate place.

The proper place for *grading* is at the *end* of the process of reading and responding to student papers, not at the beginning. This process should begin with *reading*.

You can't accurately respond to or fairly evaluate something you haven't read. The grade you assign, in the end, reduces the complex qualities of written communication to a single value, and you can assess those qualities only through reading the paper as an attempt to communicate. In turn, you can respond effectively only as a reader. If someone sent you a letter and you returned it with a grade of B+ justified by a brief comment (such as "You have some good ideas, but your letter needs to be reorganized with the main idea stated in the first paragraph"), the writer would be dissatisfied and justifiably offended. Yet this is the kind of response that most student writers have learned to expect and settle for, from teachers who are primarily *grading* their papers.

Teachers usually think of themselves as graders from the beginning of the process because they think grading is the end: the ultimate goal. Like most student writers, they want to be done with the process from the moment they begin, so compressing all the dimensions of the process (reading, commenting, correcting, evaluating) into a single operation seems the most efficient way to get the job done. But making grades a primary goal of reading papers is not necessarily the most efficient approach, and doing so has a number of unfortunate effects.

The Effects of Reading with Grading as a Goal

- Doing so encourages student writers to believe that "the grade is all that really matters." They learn to think of their own writing not as a form of communication but as an object of evaluation.

- However important they might be as symbols of accomplishment, grades don't say very much about writing, and teachers who are primarily grading don't tend to say much about writing either. Their responses become justifications of the grade, reduced to the impoverished, binary language of evaluation: *good/bad, right/wrong, strong/weak, successful/unsuccessful.* When we feel we should translate our responses as readers into the voice of a grader, that translation usually carries us in the wrong direction and is a waste of time.

- As you move through the paper, grading as you read will tend to produce fragmented comments and corrections that replace or distract from thoughtful comments on the whole piece or general suggestions for revision.

- While reading student papers receptively to find out what they have to say can be interesting, grading or "correcting" papers is usually a tedious, frustrating process.

Teachers who evaluate and mark papers while they read do so for a variety of reasons that correspond with very different styles of "grading papers." Efficiency is one of these motives, but not the only one. In fact the most inefficient methods fall into this general category as well. The following are three recognizable types of graders, with distinct motives and methods.

- *The grading machine.* Teachers who are really just grading papers read only to determine the grade, which they usually place at the end, sometimes with a general comment or two. Such teachers often approach an essay as though it were a multiple-choice exam, searching for certain "points" — right or wrong answers. Reading essentially as optical scanners, they make few marks in the text, if any, or leave little check marks in the margins. Students often ask us, "What do those little check marks mean?" Suggesting that they simply register the grader's passage through the paper, one student referred to these checks as "grader droppings"; another called them "tracks."

- *The instructive grader.* More conscientious teachers read papers in an instructive frame of mind. Because they want most of all to be helpful, they pause to provide comments, corrections, and questions in the text while they read, along with more general summary comments and suggestions at the end. This style of grading is standard, traditional practice for professional writing teachers and for other teachers who hope to improve student writing. Comments in the text and margins might include leading questions about the substance of the paper (*Is this the only explanation Banks offers?*); notation of errors (*sentence fragment*); praise (*Good point!*); or notes on writing style (*awkward sentence; use the active voice; wrong word*), sometimes marked in editorial code (*awk; pass.; ww*).

- *The copy editor.* While they read, the most thorough graders feel compelled to mark and correct everything that conflicts with their own literary tastes and standards. They correct, or at least mark, errors in spelling, punctuation, and grammar. They cross out and rewrite sentences, rearrange information in paragraphs, substitute words, and point out false statements and misconceptions. These teachers really want to rewrite the paper or to show the student in detail how it should have been written.

Here is a sample of the work the grader as copy editor might produce:

makes
What ~~kind of characteristic must~~ a teacher ~~have to be con-~~

~~sidered as a~~ good ~~teacher~~ or a poor ~~teacher~~? There are many
separate teachers   *distinct*
ways to ~~differentiate a teacher~~ into ~~two simple~~ categories. The

question is, what are two words that best differentiate~~s~~ ~~two~~

terms

~~different~~ teachers? I believe ~~that~~ the ~~best words are~~ "Effec-

tive" and "Ineffective"/ *are preferable.*

   When classifying   *s*

~~In order to put a~~ teacher ~~in a certain category~~, there are

various aspects to consider such as

~~a lot of things to cover.~~ Intelligence, personality, education,/~~and~~

             Finding   *which covers*   *of above*

~~etc. In order to find~~ a word ~~that consist~~ all the subjects

is nearly impossible

~~mentioned above would be even more difficult. How about in-~~

~~telligent and ignorant?~~ The words "Intelligent" and "Ignorant,"

for example, refer to   *intelligence; the terms*

~~only deals with~~ a teacher's ~~brains. How about~~ "Happy" and

    refer   *to*

"Grim"? ~~These words~~ only ~~deals with the~~ personality ~~aspect of~~

          "Effective," however, a wide variety of characteristics.

~~the teacher.~~ The word "~~Caring~~" ~~best~~ describes ~~all aspects~~.

   [new paragraph]

Of these three ways of grading papers, *instructive grading* is by far the most useful to student writers, who can sometimes find in specific and general comments a pattern that will improve their work on the following assignments. Because the specific comments in the text occur in the process of reading, however, they will not clearly indicate patterns unless the final comments point to these patterns in retrospect. Some of the efficiency gained in reading and responding at once will be lost, in terms of value to the student, in the clutter of particulars.

This loss is much greater in the case of *copy editing*: the most inefficient method of responding to student work. However virtuous and dutiful your reasons for falling into the practice of line editing, most of that labor will be lost on your students. Those who will not rewrite the paper will simply register the mass and weight of your corrections in relation to the grade, without looking closely, and will perhaps conclude that they need to do better next time — a value you could have gained simply by saying, *This paper is error-ridden and disorganized. You need to do better next time.* Those who will rewrite the paper will simply make all of your corrections that they can decipher because you have, in effect, assumed responsibility for the quality of their work.

> *An important exception:* Used with the methods we suggest later, line editing a single paragraph or passage can be a useful way to point out specific patterns of error, the need for sentence revision or paragraph reorganization, and problems of style. If you refer to this edited portion in your final comments, as an example of the work that needs to be done in the whole paper, you can give students the benefit of careful editing without assuming full responsibility for revision.

What Students Prefer

Teachers often feel that they are primarily graders because they assume that undergraduates are most concerned about the grades on their papers. The emphasis attached to this assumption feeds a self-fulfilling prophecy.

When we ask undergraduates what kinds of responses they really want, however, they tell us they are not satisfied even by a high grade without thoughtful responses from their teachers. Instead, students who care at all about their work want indications that their papers have been read, as pieces of communication, by a real human being, who then responds as a reader. They realize that their teachers might be very busy readers who don't have time to reply at length or in great detail. But they appreciate any response that answers their lingering questions when they turn in a paper: *How did the paper work? Did you understand what I was trying to say? What do you think of it?*

Our anecdotal evidence is supported by extensive long-term research on student writers conducted by Nancy Sommers and her staff at Harvard University. Based on studies of more than four hundred undergraduates through their four years at Harvard, this research indicated that students value thoughtful feedback as an essential part of the writing process and as a foundation for their development. One of the participants in the study noted, "Everyone told me that I would feel anonymous at college, but the feedback made me feel as if someone was paying attention to me, reading my work, making me feel seen and heard." In turn, Sommers found, "Students report feeling insulted and angry when they receive little or no feedback on their writing" ("Responding" 2). The overwhelming majority of these undergraduates wanted more detailed feedback on their papers, including guidance on drafts and earlier stages of the writing process.

Regardless of length and detail in the feedback, however, students most valued thoughtful replies that engaged them in dialogue with teachers who had made an effort to understand what they were saying.

According to the study, some of the most useful types of comments were

- questions that stimulated further thought
- brief summaries of what the reader got out of the paper
- descriptions of difficulties the reader encountered
- even highly critical feedback that was constructive and respectful

All of these preferred responses presumed that the teacher had thoroughly read and tried to understand a particular paper as an attempt to communicate and was not simply registering its points of correspondence or misalignment with a grading template.

> College students are in some ways very sensitive and respon-
> sive to their teachers' real aims and methods. In the interests
> of getting higher grades, meeting expectations, and using their
> own time more efficiently, they will adopt the values your grad-
> ing style seems to emphasize and reward.

If you habitually read and respond to essays as if they were dumping
grounds for facts and points to be checked off, your students will dump
into their essays everything they know, with the assumption that you
will find a relevant point if it is in there somewhere.

In other words, students' aims and motives as writers will adapt to
your aims and motives as a reader of their work, and you cannot expect
good writing to matter to them if it does not appear to count in your
approach to response.

A Basic Method for Responding to Student Writing

Everything we have said thus far suggests a way to approach the stack
of papers you have received for evaluation.

1. *First sit back and read through each paper receptively, letting it
communicate whatever it is trying to say.*

And do so, we sometimes advise teachers, "with your hands behind
your back," resisting the temptation to comment and correct while you
read. An effective piece of writing should engage your attention at the
beginning, tell you where it is going (or at least clearly turn you in that
direction), and carry you smoothly toward a destination or conclusion.
While you are reading, therefore, you can register the extent to which
the writing has those effects on you, along with the places where you
get confused or lost, run into a patch of fog, remain unconvinced, or get
sidetracked. Do you arrive, finally, at a real destination, or back where
you started, or at some illogical conclusion, or nowhere at all? To keep
track of these effects and other responses, you can make notes on a
separate page.

2. *Compose a reply to the writer as a set of organized comments at
the end of the paper, on the back, or on a separate page.*

Here are some suggestions for composing your response:

- Reply to the writer of the paper in your own voice as the
  intended reader.

- Begin with the general and move to the specific. It is often a
  good idea to begin by summarizing what you believe to be the
  purpose and/or argument of the essay; you can then assess
  the means by which it successfully got its message across;
  and finally, suggest possible improvements in two or three of
  the most important areas. Or you might begin with what
  you've determined to be "the heart of the matter": the most

important thing you would need to say if you could say only one thing. To the extent that you can, then explain in greater detail what you mean or point out a couple of other issues or patterns. Or you might decide to concentrate on issues you have been emphasizing in class as important to this paper, such as the development of counterarguments or the definition of terms.

- Put your reply in the form of a short letter or note, addressed directly to the writer. Even if it is very brief, you should write legibly in full sentences. We can't expect our students to value complete, continuous, coherent writing if we reply in scrawled fragments and codes (*Nice job but some frag's — see WR, G5*).

- Take the time occasionally to reread your end comments. What will the student learn from your response? How might it affect the student's future work? Does it recognizably describe the paper you have just read, in terms that acknowledge what this student had to say about this subject? Have you avoided making comments about the writer's character or work habits, distinguishing between the paper and the student? Is your tone that of a friendly ally or of an exasperated and exhausted target of deliberately bad writing?

Even in response to unsuccessful papers, constructive criticism will identify the potential for better work, in a receptive tone.

Two Sample End Comments on Weak Papers

The following are comments on a paper on what makes writing interesting in social research, from a sociology course on social research literature:

Anthony,

I really enjoyed reading this as far as it went, but it didn't seem to get finished for some reason, or perhaps it ended up illustrating the very problem it tried to describe. The notion that real communication originates with the self, and that fully public discourse is banal, is very interesting — perhaps even partly true. But it certainly limits the potential of language in situations that are not "intimate." How do you account for the value of academic writing, for example, or find reasons to produce it as a student writer?

I'm genuinely curious. As the subject of your essay moves from private toward public discourse, your own writing diminishes, becomes less vivid, and finally vanishes altogether. You can see this change in the length of paragraphs and sentences and in the qualities of language. How can you restore balance and sustain the lively voice with which you began?

The following are comments on a hypothetical *Science News* release on solar neutrino research developments, from an astrophysics course:

Roberto,

I truly like your idea: detecting neutrinos by running the nuclear reactions in reverse. This is very clever and you are right to build your article around it. As a news article on this important development, however, your account lacks narrative flow and engagement. After all, it is your job to communicate, and you might as well make this as easy and interesting as possible.

The narrative flow is sometimes broken by information that seems out of place — for instance, where you cite the cost of the project and where you say "brings into question the origins of the universe." In both cases there is no buildup beforehand or explanation afterward. Can you find other spots where the same thing happens?

And because your idea is exciting, you should treat it accordingly. Believe me, if there were evidence that the sun were generating energy twice as fast as people thought, we would go through the roof! Yet you don't seem very excited about your fascinating results and don't present them with the drama they deserve. And a sense of drama is, again, partly a matter of narrative flow: organization.

3. *When you have written the final comments, go back to the student's text and insert specific questions, suggestions, or praise. Try to limit most of these points to illustrations of things you have said in the final comments.*

You can often do this most efficiently by numbering (or otherwise coding) specific points in your final comments and inserting those numbers beside relevant examples in the text. Some teachers simply note in the comments that they have underlined or circled examples of the pattern they have described: ambiguous sentences, assertions that need supporting evidence, ideas that deserve further emphasis, points that could be developed in revision, especially fluent passages, or types of errors. Pointing out a passage that works exceptionally well can be the most valuable response, because such a passage represents a model of the standards the student is already capable of reaching.

4. *Then, if necessary, determine the grade.*

When you have completed the previous three stages, you should know (as well as you can ever know) what grade the paper deserves. You can embed the grade into your end comments, as part of your general assessment — especially if you are writing your comments on a computer, so that last-minute changes are possible. Here are some tips for grading:

- Use (and share) your criteria. If you have done a good job of planning and presenting the essay assignment (see Chapter 2), students will know what criteria they were to meet in a particular piece of writing, and you will have your own guide to evaluating their texts. Some instructors, besides making clear the expectations for each essay, also share their overall criteria for what constitutes an A, B, and so on, for papers written for their courses. This guide, in addition to guiding students, can help when it's time to decide on grades.

- Avoid mathematical systems. For reasons that may be self-evident at this point, we do not as a rule recommend determining the grade for individual papers through a system of points: 50 points for content, 20 for organization, 20 for use of evidence, and 10 for sentence correctness. Such systems, in design and execution, are at best arbitrary, and the categories rarely can be cleanly separated. Most instructors find themselves, in fact, manipulating points in order to achieve the grade they want to assign. Best just to assign a grade, knowing that your comments will distinguish the factors on which the grade is based.

- Determine (and announce) your grading policies early. It's a good idea to announce a policy concerning paper grades, late papers, grades for informal writing and drafts, participation, and the course grade on the first day of class, *in writing*. It's always easy to become more lenient; it is very difficult (even wrong) to get tough or establish a policy once the course is under way.

- Keep a careful record of grades, required work other than final essays, attendance, and anything else that will affect a student's ultimate success or lack of it. If you keep careful records and stick to an announced policy, you shouldn't have to worry about challenges to your grades; even more important, you will notice when a student is in trouble early enough to do something about it.

- Be prepared for occasional challenges to your grades. Students do have a right to question grades they consider unfair, and we have a responsibility to consider their reasons. As a matter of policy, however, we refuse to discuss a student's vague discontent or insinuations that the grade on a paper might be too low. In these cases we immediately ask students to explain to us in writing why they believe the grade is too low. Such requests give them further opportunity to demonstrate their skills at reasoned argument. But they rarely use this opportunity.

Using (and Saving) Time Wisely

The approach we have described is a fairly efficient and very effective way to read and respond to papers in a small writing class or in another kind of course with fifteen or twenty students. But advice of general value to teachers should also apply to much larger courses, where you may have forty papers or more to read in a week, in the midst of other responsibilities. For each four- or five-page paper the steps we outlined might take thirty minutes or more, and this could be more time than you have.

You can, however, adapt the method we have described for responding to student writing to a wide range of circumstances and course sizes if you keep some basic principles and techniques in mind:

- Give reading essays priority over grading them.

- Avoid line editing and random, reactive comments in the text. But make very brief, general comments (*Proofread carefully for typos and spelling. The last paragraph is just a summary, not a conclusion*) that accurately alert the writer to matters of special concern to you.

- Respond to key issues you have identified and emphasized in advance as important. Perhaps write these up as a short list to ensure that you address them in each essay. This procedure will save you time in deciding what to comment on.

- Respond to the writer as a reader, in final comments that emphasize the most important features of the paper.

- When you return to the text, to the extent that you have time, limit yourself to comments you can be reasonably sure the writer can understand and put to use.

These principles and techniques remain important because teachers often waste the most time in their responses to papers when they have the least time and feel rushed. Comments they make in the text become haphazard reactions. Final comments become empty, habitual generalizations (*A good job overall, but there is room for improvement*). Spending more time on the first papers they read, they run out of time later and mark papers with increasing haste. As they tire and become rushed, their responses and evaluations become inconsistent.

If you keep our principles in mind and first determine how much time you can spend on each paper, you can then develop a strategy for using that time most effectively and consistently. These deliberate methods will be almost invariably more efficient than the ones you simply fall into without thinking. If you remember that students want most of all to know how the paper worked for you as a reader and how it could be improved, your most important task is to convey that message first, even if it is the only thing you have time to say. If you have more time, you can elaborate that response.

Here are some further suggestions for adapting our strategies to your own circumstances and inclinations:

- Before writing any comments, skim the entire batch of papers (or read at least three or four) to gather a sense of the range of approaches and qualities you are likely to encounter and to create a clearer basis for evaluating individual papers.

- As you read through a batch of papers, begin to make a list of common patterns and problems. Rather than repeating the same comments on many of the papers, you can explain these patterns in a handout to all of the students.

- If problems in a paper are baffling or require complex instruction, simply note the general issue and ask the student to see you during office hours to discuss the problem.

- More generally, think of your responses not as the last and only word on the student's writing but as part of a broader dialogue that might include discussion during or after class, e-mail exchanges, or conferences. Nancy Sommers's Harvard study indicated that undergraduates greatly appreciate that dialogue, which makes written evaluation less a form of absolute judgment.

- For related reasons, one of our colleagues asks each of his students to buy a tape cassette, tape-records his responses to their papers, and returns the cassettes with their papers so they can hear what he has to say. He finds that he can say more in less time, his comments are literally voiced in ways that humanize the process, and his students pay closer attention to his spoken response.

- Limit yourself to two or three important observations and make them as clear as possible. Students are more likely to register a couple of strong messages than a litter of disconnected comments.

- It is almost always more efficient and effective to return responsibility for the writing to the writer than to assume that responsibility yourself. For example, if you are bothered by numerous spelling errors, do not correct them or even mark them with *sp.* Instead, you might count them in a passage and just say, *There are ten spelling errors on the first page alone.* If the writers care at all, they will try to find those errors; if they don't care, correcting their spelling will not solve the problem. Questions (*Does this conclusion follow from your argument?; Where does Locke actually say this?*) are also efficient ways to return responsibility to the writer. Descriptions of your experience as a reader (*I could follow your argument easily until page 3, where I got hopelessly lost*) have similar effects.

- Even if you do not assign revisions, keep copies of your comments on papers, so you can recall your advice and keep track of changes in a student's work. Writing comments on a computer or as e-mail messages makes this easier and saves a lot of paper.

In Chapter 9 we offer more detailed accounts of these and other methods for including and evaluating writing in large classes.

Breaking the Silence: The Student's Role in Response

We have thus far assumed that when students bring completed papers to class, you will fulfill your conventional role by collecting these papers, reading and evaluating them outside class time, and returning them with your comments and grades. Although this is what students will expect you to do, there are interesting and time-saving alternatives.

For example, this conventional role presumes that evaluating the writing is entirely your job and that the writers' own perceptions of their work, including their doubts and dissatisfactions, become irrelevant when they turn in their papers. You are supposed to tell them how well their papers worked with the assumption that they don't know, when in fact students often do know quite clearly or have false perceptions you should know about.

Why not ask *students* what they think of their work before they turn it in?

Students are surprisingly honest in their self-assessments, probably because a cost/benefit analysis favors honesty. In other words, praising a paper they know is flawed might invite your criticism; emphasizing weaknesses might have the same effect. As a consequence, students will often give you very useful assessments, along with the reasons for which they are dissatisfied with their work, such as *I know the paper falls apart at the end, but I was running out of time and couldn't find a way to tie it all together*, or *My summary of Dawkins sounds wrong somehow, but I really had trouble understanding the reading.*

This exercise takes very little class time and can save you a lot of time and guesswork when you later read and comment on the papers. If the writers do recognize their own strengths and weaknesses, you can simply reply, *I agree completely with your assessment. Those changes will greatly improve the paper.* If they recognize a problem but don't know how to resolve it, you can offer very focused advice. If they fail to see central problems or imagine problems you do not see, you can address those conflicts in your comments.

The Student Response Exercise, and Variations

The Basic Approach

- In class, before students turn in their papers, ask them to look over their work quickly and write a note to you on the back — along with notes in the text if they like — explaining the strengths and weaknesses they see or ways the paper could be improved.

Variations

- Ask students to tell you in their notes what they think you will say about their papers.

- Ask them to tell you what changes they would make if they had two more days to work on their papers.

- Tell them to respond to the previous question on a separate piece of paper, collect only those notes (so you will know what they said they would do), and without collecting the papers give them two more days to revise.

- If you want to see the original version and offer guidance, collect the papers and the notes, reply to the notes with further suggestions and changes, and give them two more days to revise.

- You can conduct the exercise out of class. When you collect the papers, tell students to send you e-mail messages explaining the changes they would like to make, and reply to them by e-mail. (Students need not receive back the papers because they are, of course, stored on their computers.)

- You can also break the silence of paper submission (or make this submission less submissive) by asking pairs of students to exchange papers, read them, and make written suggestions for revision on the back or on separate pages. For this exercise there are also variations, similar to those above. You can give the writer time to reply to the reader's suggestions; you can also conduct this exchange out of class through e-mail messages, copied to you.

All of these options encourage the treatment of student writing as communication between and among human beings, in human voices, with mutual acknowledgment that the complex qualities of written language cannot be (or in any case should not be) reduced to evaluative codes.

4

Assigning and Responding to Revision

Key Elements

Undergraduate Visions of Writing: First Draft as Last Draft   64

The effort of undergraduates to make the first draft the last accounts for many weaknesses we observe in their writing. These are not just the symptoms of weak writing ability; they are more fundamentally the characteristics of first drafts, including most of our own.

Two Kinds of Revision   64

We need to recognize that the term *revision* refers to changes writers make at different stages of the writing process and for different reasons. In the first stage, writers make changes to complete a draft before they give it to the intended reader; in the second, writers are obliged to make changes after they have submitted a draft with the hope that it is finished. Most student writing seems unfinished because the writer has never lingered in the first stage of writing, during which revision usually takes place for experienced writers.

Revision before Submission of a Draft   66

We need to delay the sense of completion that weds writers to the ideas and language they first used. For this purpose we can create circumstances in which writing in the early stages of the process remains unfinished, malleable, and expendable, as work in progress. Some ways to assign writing as a work in progress include

- informal, preparatory writing to delay the production of a draft
- writing *about* the paper
- proposals and introductions to the paper
- counterarguments

Revision after Submission of a Draft 67

If you want students to rewrite a completed draft, not just to correct it, you need to get the draft dismantled — open to reconstruction — in the mind of the writer. Some methods to achieve this include eliciting students' written plans for revision, using peer review for motivation and guidance, grading portfolios of papers, and respecting the draftiness of drafts.

Responding to Drafts for Revision 68

When responding to drafts, open these versions of the papers to revision, with guidance for making improvements. Comments for revision should

- illuminate the apparent argument and structure of the draft
- offer comments about strengths and about further possibilities
- identify fundamental limitations and problems
- leave the task of solving those problems to the writer

Strategies in End Comments for Eliciting Revision 70

In-Class Work on Revision 71

Sometimes it may be appropriate to address issues of revision with your entire class.

- Bring in samples of revision to discuss.
- When you have returned a batch of drafts, ask students to begin revision in class.
- Ask students to bring all their essays from the course to class. Have them review and summarize your comments.

Methods for Structuring Peer Review 72

Like the value of other teaching strategies, the value of peer review will depend on the way you structure and supervise the activity, in line with the design and goals of your class.

Suggestions for In-Class Peer Review 73

Suggestions for Out-of-Class Peer Review 75

Undergraduate Visions of Writing:
First Draft as Last Draft

All professional writers, including scholars, know that good writing usually results from extensive revision, often with the help of friends, colleagues, and peer reviewers in the process. As a professor in the sciences once told us, "A first draft confronts you with the nature of your own confusion on the subject. Revision gives you a chance to recover from that confusion." In other words, first thoughts on a topic aren't often our best thoughts, and "re-vision" offers us the opportunity to look at the matter again, from a different angle. Most of us find this process frustrating at times, but we know from experience that first drafts rarely meet standards for professional scrutiny and publication. Fluent, thoughtful, polished writing may sound as though the author produced it at one sitting, without hesitation. But like all fine performance, good writing conceals its own history and hides the effort required to produce that sense of effortless expression.

Because they see only the products of this labor, undergraduates tend to assume that the fluency and cohesion of the published writing they read in their courses results from the sheer brilliance or inspiration of talented, experienced authors, not from painstaking revision. In her studies of the writing strategies of college freshmen, Nancy Sommers found that these students thought of writing as something akin to inspired, unrevisable speech. With this conception of writing, they confined alterations of their papers to editorial substitutions, deletions, and corrections. In fact, they did not use the term *revision* because they did not really revise ("Revision"). We have further evidence that when left to their own devices the majority of undergraduates attempt to complete their papers (even long research papers) in a single draft, without major changes in the ideas and organization.

This effort of undergraduates to make the first draft the last accounts for many weaknesses we observe in their writing, including shallow and narrow perspectives, internal contradictions, loose organization, awkward sentences, and a stiff, demonstrative style that results from the writer's struggle to assemble first thoughts into something that sounds thought-through. These are not just the symptoms of weak writing ability; they are more fundamentally the characteristics of first drafts, including most of our own.

Two Kinds of Revision

If avoidance of revision causes many of these problems in student writing, asking students to revise their papers would appear to offer the solution. The results, however, are often disappointing. When we simply give students the opportunity to revise their papers, without detailed guidance, they tend to make only the cosmetic, editorial changes

Sommers described. When we offer detailed suggestions, student writers tend to confine their revisions to the changes we recommend, leaving us in the awkward position of evaluating the fruits of our own labor. Peer reviews from other students often yield haphazard or superficial revisions, and monitoring these reviews adds substantially to our workload. Because all of these procedures are time-consuming, teachers often decide that the costs of assigning revision outweigh the benefits.

To understand what is going wrong, we need to recognize that the term *revision* refers to changes writers make at different stages of the writing process and for different reasons. Two categories of revision, made at two stages of writing, present the sharpest contrasts:

- *First stage:* The changes writers make in order to complete a draft before they give it to the intended reader

- *Second stage:* The changes writers are obliged to make after they have submitted a complete draft, with the hope that it is finished

Most of the revision teachers assign is of the second type, which corresponds with the suggestions we receive from editors and peer reviewers on manuscripts for publication. And in that stage of the process, most of us respond to suggestions as our students do: we change what we can't avoid changing.

For individual writers, therefore, the willingness to revise is not a constant. Instead, this motivation changes with differing circumstances and at different stages of the writing process. We can better understand these variations if we think of writing as a substance that "sets up" at some point in the process, like concrete. Beyond that point, when language and thought have lost malleability, extensive changes require something on the order of dynamite.

Delaying this point of solidification, most experienced writers revise their work extensively, as a malleable substance, *before* they submit a complete draft. Student writing, by contrast, tends to set up almost at the moment it hits the page, as a linear sequence of words and sentences. "It's exactly like building a wall," a Cornell freshman said, explaining why he does not revise. "You can't take anything out once you've put it in. I think that each sentence is something I really wanted to express, and just to take it out is like . . . like breaking the wall down."

First thoughts thus become last thoughts, and second thoughts seem disruptive. So do teachers' comments that require extensive changes to a paper the writer considers virtually finished.

Most student writing seems unfinished, in other words, because it is finished too soon. The student has never lingered in the first stages of writing during which revision usually takes place for experienced writers.

Why do undergraduates try to make the first draft the last? From her research on college freshmen, Nancy Sommers concluded that "it is not that students are unwilling to revise, but rather that they do what they have been taught to do in a consistently narrow and predictable way" ("Revision" 383). Learned, linear procedures such as constructing and following outlines can discourage writers from altering the viewpoint and organization of their papers.

In our own investigations, however, undergraduates most often say that they try to complete papers in one draft because they have neither the time nor the motivation to revise their work. When their teachers assign finished papers with tight deadlines in the midst of other homework and exams, students tell us, the most efficient way to complete the assignment is to begin with the intention of producing only one draft. As a junior said, when describing the process of writing a thirteen-page research paper, "Right from the beginning I knew that my first draft was going to be my last." She did not revise the ideas or organization of this paper, she explained, "because they were already determined before I started writing." She attributed this approach both to "time constraints" and to a "sense of completion" that substantial revision would disrupt.

These explanations suggest that the circumstances in which we typically assign writing discourage students from revising their work before they turn it in, as finished writing. And if they view assigned "drafts" as virtually finished products (like submitted manuscripts), our students will be reluctant to revise those drafts beyond the changes we prescribe. If we want undergraduates to view revision as a normal, essential part of the writing process, therefore, we must create circumstances in which revision seems normal and necessary.

Because revisions before and after the submission of a draft occur in different circumstances, with different goals, we will discuss these types of revision separately.

Revision before Submission of a Draft

If students avoid revising first drafts (and first thoughts) because their writing sets up too quickly, we need to delay that "sense of completion" that weds writers to the ideas and language they first used. For this purpose we can create circumstances in which writing in the early stages of the process remains unfinished, malleable, and expendable, as work in progress.

Ways to Assign Writing as Work in Progress

Most types of informal and preparatory writing that we will describe in Chapter 5 serve this purpose of delaying the production of a final draft. The "writing to learn" activities we list there (such as reflective journals, study questions, and reading notes) support specific purposes of learning, but they also produce material for further writing through extensive revision. Workshops on paper topics, written debates, groundwork assignments, and other "preparations for performance" either generate or encourage revision of early drafts.

Here are some other, related ways to assign writing as work in progress:

- *Assign writing **about** the paper.* If you assign a "draft" of a paper, students will still attempt to produce the finished product with the hope that serious revision won't be necessary. Instead, you can establish the tentative, exploratory nature of a first draft if you ask students to write at some length *about* the ideas, arguments, and evidence they are considering for their papers. Writing *about* the paper ensures that students do not think of this work as the final version.

- *Assign introductions to the paper before a draft is due.* These introductions should include the central question, thesis, or argument the paper will address and might include an outline of the supporting points and evidence that will follow. This material is especially useful for work in small groups or in paired exchanges outside class. In response to your comments as well, writers are more likely to make significant changes to early portions of a draft than to full versions of the paper.

- *Assign multiple proposals or introductions.* First thoughts can't be last thoughts if students have to come up with more than one. Two or three options will also give you more room for constructive advice. You won't have to invent alternatives if one proposal doesn't work, and you can suggest combinations of approaches.

- *Assign counterarguments.* When students have proposed or drafted an argument, ask them to describe the most effective counterarguments. In the next version, they should take these other views into account, either by reformulating the original argument or by addressing the opposing points. Students can also do this work in pairs, writing counterarguments to each other's draft either in or outside the class.

Revision after Submission of a Draft

Through the lens of grading, teachers often view revision as a second chance for students to produce solid, fluent papers that will receive good grades. Accordingly, they ask students to turn in papers that they will have the opportunity to change and resubmit before they receive grades. For reasons we have explained, however, when writers have reached a sense of completion, they are reluctant to make substantial changes beyond the ones teachers or publishers directly tell them to make. At this stage, voluntary, undirected revision rarely yields major improvements, and detailed instructions usually involve more work for the teacher than for the writer.

If you want students to rewrite completed drafts, not just to correct them, you need to get the draft dismantled — open to reconstruction — in the mind of the writer. Skillful comments can do some of this disassembly, as we will observe in the next section of this chapter. But there are other strategies for motivating writers to make serious revisions on their own, even when they hope the task is finished.

Strategies for Eliciting Revision of Drafts

- *Elicit students' written plans for revision.* Students are more likely to undertake extensive revisions if they have first described the changes they need to make. Written plans for revision, following your comments or peer review, become an informal contract for the new version. And if writers do not do the work they propose, this document will be a useful reference in your evaluation of the final draft.

- *Use peer review for motivation and guidance.* Students can be of great help to one another in providing guidance for revision of drafts if they have guidelines for peer review, which we will discuss in the last section of this chapter. If the writers receive two or more reviews of a paper from other students, their written plans for making use of this advice will be especially helpful. Such statements of intention from writers are required in many peer-reviewed journals.

- *Grade portfolios of papers.* Portfolio systems postpone the finality of grading because they allow students to revise their work extensively before the portfolios are evaluated at the end of the term, and in some courses also at midterm. In most cases students submit assigned drafts at scheduled times, but further revisions remain open possibilities until the portfolios are graded.

- *Respect the draftiness of drafts.* To remain open to revision, a draft should represent a tentative, exploratory approach to the subject. But teachers often read and respond to first drafts as flawed versions of the finished product, even when they have assigned "rough" drafts. Students then feel penalized for loose ends or undeveloped ideas and revert to caution.

Responding to Drafts for Revision

The purposes of responding to finished papers (for evaluation) and to drafts (for revision) differ in important ways that teachers need to keep in mind:

- When responding to finished papers, let the writers know how well their papers worked and offer suggestions that might be useful in future projects.

- When responding to drafts, open these versions of the papers to revision, with guidance for making improvements.

If you want to avoid doing most of the revising yourself, however, you should refrain from being *too* helpful. Extremely helpful and extremely critical teachers share the tendency to tell students in detail what is wrong with their papers and how the problems can be fixed. In other words, they think of response as "correcting papers." Students who are simply following instructions learn most of all how skillful their teachers are at revising drafts.

If you want your students to learn how to revise their own work, you need to stimulate their motivation to make changes and leave the primary responsibility for revision with them. If you pause to consider what you are doing, you can probably sense when you are assuming the responsibility for revision, through copy editing or giving detailed instructions. Limited amounts of prescriptive and corrective advice can be useful, or even necessary when students can't understand specific problems on their own. If you fall into the general habit of providing instructions for revision, however, your students will fall into the habit of following those instructions. You will see further improvements in their writing only when you devote more time and attention to showing them what they should change.

Because individual students need specific kinds of help, no single type of response will always work. As a rule, however, as we noted in the previous chapter when discussing comments on essays, comments for revision should

- illuminate the apparent argument and structure of the draft

- offer comments about strengths and about further possibilities

- identify fundamental limitations and problems

- leave the task of solving those problems with the writer

Sample Commentary

The following are some of the final comments on the first draft of a report on the religious affiliations of Korean students, written for a course on social research.

David,

I'll start by explaining what remains mysterious to me in your report on a fascinating study of changing religious affiliations among Korean students. Although you interviewed ten students, synopses of only five interviews appear here. And although these were apparently long interviews — between 30 and 90 minutes — some of the accounts of them are extremely short, as though there wasn't much content. I should add that these accounts are nicely written and interesting in themselves — especially the interview with C, which is full and beautifully composed with a mixture of quotations, paraphrases, and explanations. As the paper progresses they remain nicely composed, but get shorter, as though there was less and less to say.

I realize that this is a draft and that you probably had trouble figuring out how you could fit all this material coherently into a single paper. But when you get to the conclusions you also seem to dismiss that interview material as inconclusive, and turn back in the end to a "personal hypothesis" without reference to your data, suggesting that the whole question is confusing, unspecific to Koreans, and illogical.

Can you find patterns that allow you to use more of this rich material? If you can't, what happens if you think of inconsistency itself as a pattern, allowing you to present a greater variety of perspectives?

This example illustrates some of the following strategies for eliciting real revision.

Strategies in End Comments for Eliciting Revision

- *Describe rather than prescribe.* If you simply describe what the writers have and have not done in first drafts, they can often see gaps, contradictions, and alternatives as observations of their own that they can and should act upon. Prescriptive statements (*You need to revise your thesis*) represent *your* observations and incentives to revise.

- *Describe the experience of reading the draft.* Letting the writer know what is happening as you read can be a very efficient, effective way to stimulate revision without prescribing it. Such accounts of reading work especially well in the margins: *I could follow the argument easily to this point, but now I'm lost. I can't see how these conclusions follow from the examples above.*

- *Ask questions.* Whether in the margins or in final comments, questions function as little prybars that open the draft to further thought yet leave responsibility for finding answers with the writer. Many statements (*You need a transition here*) can be posed more effectively as questions (*What is the connection between the argument in this paragraph and the example in the next?*).

- *If possible, find the basis for revision in the draft itself.* Even very rough and undeveloped drafts usually contain some promising ideas and useful material for revision. Identifying these foundations for reconstruction allows students to retain a sense that this is their own work, with its own potential for improvement (*The most interesting argument appears in the middle of paragraph 6. What would happen if you restructure the paper around that idea?*).

- *Limit editorial and stylistic changes to examples and brief passages.* If there are problems of style and error running through the paper, simply point to a couple of examples or edit a single paragraph for illustration. Be sure that you choose sentences and paragraphs most likely to remain in the revised version. If you edit an introductory paragraph *and* suggest that the student write a new introduction, these messages will seem to conflict and the writer will probably retain the edited portions.

- *Don't be shy.* When teachers complain that students did not make serious revisions, we often find that their comments did not directly call for serious revision. In many cases, to avoid sounding discouraging they began with generous statements such as *On the whole, this paper works very well,* even when they saw major problems of logic and organization. Noting these problems on a finished paper might be read as condemnation, but on a draft they represent an opportunity to salvage the work. If your comments are evasive, you deprive writers of this opportunity.

- *Teach students to follow these same principles when responding to each other's drafts* (see "Methods for Structuring Peer Review"). Students respond with alacrity to instruction in how to comment effectively on each other's work, but they will need the following help: models (such as your own responses); definitive guidelines, preferably provided for each task of response in a handout; and practice — students will tend to avoid criticism the first couple of times. Such practice will help them learn to think more critically about the subject, and it will help them learn how to read and critique writing, a facility most will need throughout their careers and lives.

In-Class Work on Revision

Much of the discussion to this point has assumed that work on revision takes place primarily through individual essays submitted to instructors and comments returned to individual students or through individual conferences.

Sometimes, however, it may also be appropriate to address issues of revision with your entire class. Here are some methods for doing so, along with reasons for trying them.

Methods for Working on Revision in Class

- Bring in samples of revision (before-and-after models) to discuss. These can include samples from your own writing (students appreciate this); from students who are doing interesting, productive rewriting; or from published work (such as drafts of the Declaration of Independence). Students learn from concrete examples of what we mean by revision, and most are surprised at the radical changes characteristic of professionally revised prose.

- When you have returned a batch of drafts on which you've written comments, ask students to use the next 20 to 30 minutes to begin rewriting. Use this time to confer with individuals about what you meant and about what they might do.

- Ask students to bring all their essays to class. Then have them review all your comments and summarize, in writing (through lists and analysis), what they find. What are they good at? What mistakes or weaknesses appear most frequently? In what areas do they now need to work? This can be an excellent strategy if you believe students are not transferring the principles of your comments from one paper to the next. They may be surprised to find that you have repeatedly given the same advice. This activity could also take place at home; students then submit their written reports to you.

Methods for Structuring Peer Review

Peer review is an essential guide to revision in almost every field of academic publication. Because publishers do not entirely trust themselves (and scholars do not entirely trust them) to make independent decisions about the value and clarity of a manuscript, they request help from members of the intended audience. In turn, authors benefit from the advice offered by their peers, even if opinions of their work differ. Editors mediate these differences and negotiate productive changes to work in progress.

There are good reasons for extending the benefits of peer review to student writing:

- Like the editor of an article or a book, the teacher holds final authority over the revisions necessary to bring student writing to completion, but advice from the writer's peers can be very useful in this process.

- Like scholars, student writers learn from several views of their work in progress.

- Students appreciate the opportunity to read one another's responses to an assignment.

- As writers, they can also gain valuable skills from the challenge of helping other writers improve their drafts.

- The skills involved in peer review are valuable not just in the classroom, but also in most professions.

Yet teachers are often reluctant to include peer review, or often discontinue the practice, because the advice students offer one another can be shallow or misleading. Although they are the writer's peers, students are not experienced reviewers or experts in the subject of the work, and they are sometimes reluctant to offer advice that seems critical. Some student readers can be *too* critical and will feel obliged to "correct" writing that you, the teacher, consider fluent and effective. Monitoring these reviews and negotiating their differences can require more time than responding directly to drafts, without peer review.

It is certainly true that if you just ask students to review one another's drafts, without guidelines, the results will be inconsistent at best, especially on the first occasion. Some readers' comments will be confined to bland praise and empty generalization (*I thought this was a really good paper; It could be clearer in some places*). Other readers will try to correct specific phrases and sentences, ignoring general problems with organization and development. You might well conclude that the exercise was a waste of time.

Like the value of other teaching strategies, however, the value of peer review will depend on the way you structure and supervise the activity, in line with the design and goals of your class. Professional writing teachers who emphasize the writing process sometimes devote most of their class time to collaborative work on drafts, in pairs or small groups. These teachers gradually train their students to provide useful feedback at different stages of the writing process, and their students learn to assume responsibility for helping one another. From the repeated experience of giving and receiving comments, these students figure out which kinds of advice are most helpful, and they realize (as other writers do) that they can offer useful suggestions even if they struggle with their own writing projects. As students become more skillful at helping one another, peer review begins to repay the time and effort teachers spend in supervising this work. When student writers receive thoughtful, constructive suggestions from their peers, they will need less detailed commentary from their teachers.

Movement in the direction of independence from the teacher is not a dereliction of duty. Student writers *should* become less dependent on teachers and more reliant on themselves and their peers in the revision and evaluation of their work.

If you have time available for peer review in class, here are some basic requirements for making this work productive.

Suggestions for In-Class Peer Review

- Form *peer review groups of three or four*; these can work better than pairs because no one gets stuck with just one, possibly ineffective or irresponsible, reviewer. If there is insufficient time for multiple readers, have students work in pairs.

- Decide whether you want to let students determine *who will read* their drafts or if you want to choose readers for yourself. If the latter, prepare the list of who will exchange with whom in advance.

- Make sure that students bring the necessary *multiple copies of their drafts* to class for distribution to the peer readers.

- Distribute *clear, written instructions* for the kind of feedback you want reviewers to provide at that stage of the process — for instance, attention to general organization and development in an early draft, qualities of evidence and other support for an argument, revision of sentences in a work that is nearly finished. It makes good sense to provide precise lists of questions the reviewers should answer or, perhaps better yet, forms they should fill out.

- If you do not use *review forms*, tell students to *write comments on the draft*, including general comments at the end.

- Make sure the students have *time in class to discuss these comments* with each other to clarify lingering questions. If all the work is done in class, schedule ample time.

- *Be on hand* to provide assistance and resolve doubts while the students are working together in class.

- Remind students of *collegiality* — that they should provide the kinds of help they would like to receive from others.

- *Repeat these exercises* as frequently as you can throughout the term. With practice, students will become more skillful at providing and utilizing peer reviews.

Out-of-Class Peer Review

In topical courses that include writing assignments, you might not have time available for peer review in class, but these exercises also work very well outside class, much as they do in the professional review of manuscripts. In fact, some teachers use professional models for peer review in their fields, especially in advanced courses where majors become familiar with professional literature. In advanced laboratory science courses, for example, teachers sometimes organize anonymous student peer reviews of lab report drafts, according to professional guidelines, and serve as the "editors" for these manuscripts. When the student authors have received the reviews, they write letters addressed to the editor, thanking the reviewers and explaining how they plan to implement the advice in a revised report. This letter, for which most science teachers can provide models, serves as a contract or promise for making changes, which the teacher can further negotiate if necessary.

If professional models and anonymous reviews seem inappropriate for your course, you can shift most features of an in-class peer review to out-of-class activities to ensure productive work.

Suggestions for Out-of-Class Peer Review

- Require students to bring sufficient *copies* of their drafts to exchange in class.

- Distribute written review *guidelines* or forms.

- Set a *deadline* for submission of peer reviews.

- Ask that students write comments directly on the essay, fill out the form you provide, or, better yet, type up a *review letter*, following the guidelines you provide.

- Provide *time in class for students to discuss these comments* with one another, to clarify lingering questions.

- Again, *repeat* this exercise as frequently as you can throughout the term.

Like journal editors, you will need to monitor these reviews to some extent; many teachers want to see all of the peer comments before they compose their own responses to drafts. If peer review is an important part of the course, the quality of these reviews may constitute part of the final grade as well.

Although it involves more paper, along with some delay, one strategy is to ask all of the reviewers to submit copies of their comments to you. Teachers who want to avoid this additional paperwork and delay structure all or parts of the peer review process as electronic exchange. Students can exchange drafts as e-mail attachments and exchange their general comments in e-mail messages, copied to you. For sentence-level and marginal comments on work that is nearly finished, they can insert suggestions in the texts and return them as attachments. Even with these electronic exchanges, however, it is a good idea for student writers to meet to discuss the drafts. These interpersonal contacts almost always raise new issues and resolve misunderstandings.

More than any other teaching practice, peer review can help students view their writing as a malleable substance that they can shape and reshape with the help of attentive readers before they submit their work to you, the final judge of its quality. The tendency for student writing to set up prematurely, like poured concrete, results in part from the sense that the first reader of this work will be its grader. Peer review delays that moment of submission and thus extends the time when writing remains a creative process, open to substantial revision.

5

Informal and Preparatory Writing

Key Elements

Practice and Performance   77

For most undergraduates, writing has been assigned as a series of performances for potentially critical, authoritative audiences, without rehearsal. Written performance is a necessary basis for grading and necessary preparation for competitive careers. Yet in all performing arts (including athletics and scholarship) good performance results from preparation: practice, rehearsal, or coaching. It is naive, therefore, to assume that your students will write well without opportunities to prepare, or rehearse, for these performances.

As a teacher or "coach," how can you build practice and rehearsal into courses that emphasize writing?

Writing to Inform Teachers   79

Teachers often feel that they should just know, somehow, who their students are and what they need to learn. Yet students rarely volunteer information about their interests, needs, and difficulties. Here are some direct and timely ways to learn about who your students are and what is going on in class:

- Beginning-of-term questionnaires
- Written midterm course evaluations
- One-minute essays in class
- Notes on writing and thinking

Writing to Learn 80

Outside of the more traditional methods of writing to learn, like note taking on lectures and readings, other, informal writing techniques can contribute to learning:

- Reflective journals
- E-mail discussion lists
- Study questions
- Reading notes
- Concept papers

Writing in Preparation for Performance 82

Few undergraduates will produce the kind of writing you have in mind on the first try. Therefore, it is beneficial to create occasions for practice and rehearsal. These informal writing exercises can improve the quality of the formal writing you assign:

- Rough drafts (see Chapter 4)
- "Writing to learn" techniques described in the previous section
- Workshops on paper topics
- Written debates
- Alternative audiences
- Writing before reading
- Groundwork assignments
- Models for writing

Practice and Performance

In addition to their specific functions in a course as exercises in learning, the finished papers that students turn in for evaluation and grading are essentially performances. In these formal essays, research papers, or reports, students demonstrate to you, their primary audience, how well they understand the subject; the extent to which they can think through an issue, pursue a line of inquiry, or develop an argument; and their ability to convey their understanding and ideas in writing.

In a course that emphasizes writing, performance is a necessary basis for grading, and it also helps to prepare students for writing in their careers. Most of the writing that graduates complete in their professions will demonstrate to audiences of colleagues and supervisors their ability to perform their jobs, and much of that writing will be at least implicitly "graded," as a basis for performance reviews and promotions. It would be naive to assign writing only as a medium of learning or only as performance.

Analogies to music and to other performing arts will help illustrate what we mean. Imagine that students in a school of music (or theater, dance, or visual arts) were taught that performance is the means to its own end: that musicians learn to perform well entirely by performing before informed, critical audiences, without practice. Imagine that in each of these performances novice musicians must play a new piece and a new kind of music without rehearsal. And imagine that to prepare for these alarming recitals they are told only to listen to the performances of experts, read music, and read about musical performance.

Instead, music teachers know, and want their students to know, that although fine performance might seem to be effortless, it results from many hours of rehearsal, many years of practice and coaching. And these means to the ends of performance are not confined to the performing arts. Imagine that athletes were not allowed to practice before competitive events, but only watched and read about athletics. Practice, rehearsal, or coaching are essential preparations for all kinds of performance, including academic publication. Scholarly books and published articles typically result from years of education and research in the discipline, discussion with colleagues about work in progress, numerous drafts, peer review, and extensive revision.

For most undergraduates, however, writing has been a series of performances for potentially critical, authoritative audiences, without rehearsal. The great majority of their writing assignments have called for performances of certain types, submitted to teachers as finished products for evaluation and grading. And through this experience, to varying degrees, they have grown used to giving poorly rehearsed, flawed performances.

How, as a coach, can you build practice and rehearsal into courses that emphasize writing?

We have already suggested ways to design courses that encourage students to write and speak in the process of learning, and our advice on assignment sequences in Chapter 2 includes assignments that build constituent skills used to meet the demands of more complex assignments later. Further chapters will discuss ways of including revision, peer review, and staged assignments for research papers. All of these methods provide forms of practice and rehearsal for written performance.

In this chapter we will focus on types of informal, typically ungraded writing that contribute to learning, stimulate informed discussion, and sometimes lead to formal papers or revisions. Although informal writing often has multiple functions, we can roughly categorize types of informal writing according to their main purposes, with some examples of each type.

Writing to Inform Teachers

Teachers often feel that they should just know, somehow — through experience, authority, or intuition — who their students are and what they need to learn. Rarely volunteering information about their individual interests, needs, and difficulties, students help maintain this shaky assumption that we have all the information we need to teach effectively. Through formal writing, exams, conferences, and discussions we gradually become more familiar with our students and the ways in which they learn. But there are more direct, timely ways of finding out who students are and what is really going on in the class, from their perspective.

Ways to Use Writing to Learn about Your Students

- *Beginning-of-term questionnaires* can give you some immediate information about your students and will let them know that you are interested in them as individuals. In addition to basic information (such as their e-mail addresses, majors, and hometowns), you can ask about particular interests, motives, and needs relevant to your teaching:

  What are your main reasons for taking this course?

  What do you hope to get out of it by the end of the term?

  What are your academic interests and career goals?

  What other courses are you taking this term?

  What other writing courses (or courses in this field) have you taken?

  What reading in this field have you done?

  What kinds of writing and reading do you prefer?

  Are there particular difficulties with writing you hope to overcome?

  What experience do you have with languages other than English?

  Is there anything you would like me to know that will help me, as your instructor?

- *Written midterm course evaluations* allow students to give you feedback on the way the course is working and particular difficulties they encounter. While final course evaluations are essentially post mortem, like the final grades you give students, assessments at midterm or earlier offer students a voice in the direction of the course and provide information you can use to improve teaching and learning. These evaluations work best if you tell students to write little essays in response to your questions, either in class or as take-home assignments. Like final evaluations, however, they should be anonymous.

- *One-minute essays* in class offer students the opportunity to give you immediate feedback on what they understand, find confusing, or want to know more about in response to the course material. Teachers often leave time for students to write these notes and collect them at the end of a class period, when thoughts and questions are fresh. These notes (which are more often five-minute essays) are an excellent basis for planning and continuity between classes.

- *Notes on writing and thinking* allow students to tell you how they actually think through and complete the formal writing you assign. These notes — which you can ask students to turn in with their papers or write in class — might alert you to difficulties in the writing process, confusion about the assignment, ideas that didn't appear in the finished paper, and other information that can help you address students' needs. While you can observe strengths and weaknesses in the finished papers they submit, notes about the writing process often help explain patterns and focus the guidance you offer for revisions and future assignments.

Writing to Learn

In *Writing to Learn Science and Mathematics*, Paul Connolly and Patricia Vilardi note that the term "writing to learn" acknowledges "the powerful role language plays in the production, as well as the presentation, of knowledge." Connolly and Vilardi go on to link writing to learn with "informal writing": "language that is forming a meaning," or language used as "the most important mediator of concepts we do not yet fully hold" (3–4). Such writing is therefore a medium used to grasp or construct understandings, while more formal writing might serve to demonstrate knowledge the writer has come to possess.

In this sense, notes on lectures and readings are common forms of "writing to learn." So are laboratory notebooks and other research notes used in the process of developing investigative papers. But many other kinds of informal writing contribute to learning. While teachers usually refrain from grading this writing, they usually read it as required work and often make a portion of the final grade contingent on completion of these exercises. Here we briefly describe just a few examples of this kind of writing, each with many potential variations.

Ways to Use Writing to Help Students Learn

- *Reflective journals* serve to capture what we sometimes call "hidden discourse" relevant to the class. While conventional notes on lectures and readings primarily record information, reflective journals record what students are thinking *about* this material and at once stimulate inquisitive and critical thinking that otherwise would not occur or would be forgotten.

Teachers who assign reflective journals usually ask students to write entries in a separate notebook and require certain amounts of writing each week — either entries for each class and assigned reading or a certain number of pages — and they restrict the content to varying degrees, according to their purpose. Some teachers use journals explicitly to ensure that students have thought about specific lectures and readings, as a basis for informed discussion and further writing. Others permit entries on any thoughts related to the subject of the course. Unless you want to learn a lot about your students' social lives and personal problems, you will want to distinguish these journals from diaries and limit their content to issues relevant to your course.

Most teachers collect these journals periodically and read them. Some also write comments on points of particular interest or confusion or identify promising ideas for future essays. Because the exploratory function of reflective journals depends upon some measure of privacy, entries should not be distributed to the class. If you want to use journal material in class, however, you can tell students at the beginning of the term that they will select passages for distribution and discussion or use selected ideas as a basis for brief presentations.

- *E-mail discussion lists* extend the exploratory function of reflective journals to written conversation among members of the class. At most institutions you can easily set up an exchange group that limits access to your students. In most cases, however, exchanges will be sporadic and of limited value unless you require participation. You can initiate discussions by posting specific issues or questions each week, or you can assign this task to individual students or groups.

- *Study questions* ask students to respond through informal writing to specific issues or to synthesize understandings assembled from course material. Teachers usually ask students to complete these brief responses before the class period when the topic will be discussed. This preparation can stimulate lively discussions that include everyone, and because reticent students will have thoughts on paper, you can ask them to participate with less concern for intimidating them. These written responses also facilitate small-group discussions, where students can compare positions they have developed, or formal debates. Teachers usually collect these papers at the end of the class and, if they have time, respond to the ideas they present.

- *Reading notes* are informal summaries of, or responses to, assigned readings for a particular week. Like study questions, they can be used to stimulate discussion, but their main function is to strengthen the students' understanding of and engagement with assigned texts. They will also give you a clearer sense of the ways in which students are reading and understanding the material and alert you to common points of confusion. Some teachers assign these notes in three parts: a brief summary of the author's position, an evaluative response to the position, and a discussion of the connections between the text and other course material.

- *Concept papers* ask students to explain, usually in a paragraph or two, especially important or difficult concepts essential to understanding the subject of the course. All teachers can identify concepts central to learning in their courses; experienced teachers can also identify concepts that students typically have difficulty understanding thoroughly. Students can best come to grips with these concepts by trying to explain them clearly in their own words, and their efforts will then facilitate further discussion and clarification. A biology teacher, for example, might ask students to define cell lines or to explain the relation between genetic drift and natural selection. In a political theory class, a concept paper might ask students to explain the most fundamental difference between the views of history in Marx and Hegel.

  In a large class you do not need to respond individually to these papers. When you have read them, you can address the most common misunderstandings in class or in a handout, and (with permission from the writers) you can distribute the most clear, cohesive explanations to the class.

Writing in Preparation for Performance

Because most undergraduates attempt to complete assignments in a single draft, often shortly before the deadline, few of them will produce the kind of writing you had in mind unless you create occasions for practice and rehearsal. As one of our students said, describing the kind of stage fright she experienced in unrehearsed performance, "I feel my writing should be coherent, intelligently composed, and interesting in order to reflect some of my nonexistent characteristics." How can we help students to bring these characteristics into existence?

Rough drafts are the most obvious forms of rehearsal for written performance, and in Chapter 4 we described ways of assigning drafts and revisions productively. Most of the writing to learn activities we have described in the previous section — reflective journals, study questions, and reading notes — can also become preparations for developing formal papers. Used to generate first thoughts on a topic, they allow emerging essays to represent further thoughts, which are usually more cohesive and interesting. Here we present a few more informal writing exercises that can improve the quality of the formal writing you assign.

Written communication relies on a sense of exchange with readers. This is especially true of argument and interpretation, in which the development of a position presumes other positions, other uses of logic and evidence. In most of the following exercises, therefore, informal writing is also a subject of discussion in classroom activities.

Ways to Use Writing in Preparation for Performance

- *Workshops on paper topics* allow students to test alternative ideas and plans for writing before they become wedded to a single approach. In small groups of three or four students, in or outside class, these discussions can focus on a variety of materials for work in progress: thesis statements, central questions the paper might address, assertions with forms of evidence, or introductory paragraphs. In each case this exercise will work best if you ask students to bring in two or more options for their paper and give the groups clear goals and procedures for discussion. In small seminars you can do some of this work with the entire class.

- *Written debates* strengthen the writer's sense that good essays must acknowledge other positions and viewpoints. To develop these exchanges, assign students different sides of an issue and ask them to draft informal arguments. Have students from opposing sides exchange drafts and write counterarguments, which the writers must acknowledge and address in revised versions. These written exchanges can also be used as a basis for classroom debates and discussion.

- *Alternative audiences* encourage students to develop arguments and explanations informally, prior to final performance, in drafts they must extensively revise. Ask students first to explain the subject or argument of their assigned paper to a familiar audience, such as a parent or a close friend, in informal language that this reader can easily understand, perhaps in the form of a letter.

- *Writing before reading* exercises encourage students to develop tentative positions on an issue before they read what authorities have to say. This preliminary work allows them to recognize the positions of other writers more easily and to write *about* those texts, rather than simply adopting the views of the authors.

- *Groundwork assignments* ask students to define central terms or to explain relevant concepts and methodologies before they begin to draft formal essays. Without this initial clarification, many papers will be based on a weak grasp of basic terms and concepts essential to their arguments and explanations.

- *Models for writing* help to prevent basic misconceptions of the forms and styles of writing your assignments require. For some assignments you can find examples of published articles, essays, reports, or reviews close to the types of work you want students to produce. In other cases you can distribute examples of effective student papers from previous terms.

Teachers are sometimes reluctant to give students models for writing because undergraduates are entirely too good at imitating the form and style of a specific essay. The exercise begins to resemble "copying" and can limit variation and creativity. Models work best, therefore, if they are first the subjects of informal writing and discussions on the general features that make this piece an example of successful writing in a form or genre used for certain purposes. Using more than one example, or referring students broadly to certain types of articles in certain publications, can also reduce slavish imitation.

We've described informal writing as varieties of practice and rehearsal that can improve the quality of performance. From a slightly different perspective, however, we can think of informal writing as a way of *delaying* performance: keeping the imminence of performance from interrupting kinds of thinking and learning that are of great value in themselves.

We know teachers in a variety of fields, from English to physics, who want to delay the finished product indefinitely and work entirely with informal, unfinished writing as a mode of learning. Teachers in an advanced biochemistry course once explained that they did not want to assign complete reports on experiments because the goals of getting significant results and reaching conclusions — goals built into the form of a finished report — interfered with the kinds of attention necessary to conduct real experiments and thus learn experimental science. For these teachers, laboratory notes are both effective and sufficient forms of writing.

For related reasons, Europeans often argue that American undergraduates are overexamined: required to perform in graded papers, examinations, quizzes, or problem sets on a weekly basis throughout the term, as though the purpose of education were to strengthen and measure short-term memory. If students are accustomed to demonstrating knowledge shortly after they get it, they will view writing as a way of getting information and ideas assembled on paper as quickly as possible.

Few of us would say that we want to teach our students to jump to conclusions, but this is what formal writing assignments often invite students to do. Informal, unfinished writing can encourage students to suspend judgment and think of both writing and learning as works in progress.

Revision, the subject of Chapter 4, can also be used for these dual purposes: to improve performance and suspend premature judgments.

6

Teaching Writing at the Sentence Level

Key Elements

Defining Terms to Clarify Instruction   87

When we talk about helping students write at the sentence level, we may have one of two quite different tasks in mind: helping students with *errors* or helping them with *style*. It can help to distinguish among important terms: mechanics, syntax (basic sentence grammar), punctuation, register, and style.

The Current State of Student Writing   88

We may ask if student writing has degenerated and if high schools have failed in their job, but a number of considerations suggest that we should modify this negative reaction.

The Recursive Nature of Learning to Write   89

Learning to write is not a linear progression. When students start to write in a new and difficult subject, they may run into trouble with sentence structure, with use of vocabulary, even with control over basic sentence correctness. Immediate and primary attention to errors or to stylistic choices may not solve the problem.

Defining Terms to Clarify Instruction

> When we talk about helping students write at the sentence
> level, we may, without realizing it, have one of two quite differ-
> ent tasks in mind. Much of the time, we're thinking about help-
> ing students avoid making mistakes. We're talking about *error*.
> We also may wish, however, to help students improve their *style*,
> a different matter altogether.

A ttending to style, we aim to help students learn how to make *choices*
about sentence patterns and diction rather than how to correct
mistakes; we're consequently apt to have a more positive mind-set.
Unfortunately, it's all too easy not to sort out which task we have in
mind and to confuse problems of error with matters of style.

We agree with the approach of a superb teacher of writing and
teaching at Cornell, Lydia Fakundiny, who urges new instructors to
get their own writing vocabularies and teaching practices straight. She
notes that teachers should distinguish among certain important terms,
as we will try to do in this chapter.

Important Terms

- *Mechanics* refers to conventions such as manuscript format,
  formats for quotations, hyphenation, underlining/italics, capitali-
  zation, spelling, and use of the apostrophe.

- *Syntax* refers to basic sentence grammar (mistakes in syntax
  would include faulty word order, errors in verb tense sequences,
  dangling modifiers — in other words, "bad grammar").

- *Punctuation* is what Fakundiny calls "an adjunct/aspect of
  syntax": punctuation is tied to the creation of meaning through
  syntactical arrangements.

- *Register* (or *usage*) indicates the degree of formality or informal-
  ity of vocabulary or syntax.

- *Style* refers to choices of words and sentence patterns; discussion
  of style can include the choice of register. It does not mean
  discussion of error in mechanics, punctuation, or syntax ("bad
  grammar").

Like Fakundiny, we hold that it is counterproductive to condemn
students for "grammatical errors" when they actually have written in
a *style* we don't approve, for instance using the passive voice where we
would choose the active. We should not criticize a student's style when
her mechanics are flawed — when the student may need, for instance,
to learn how to format quoted material.

To think about how to help students at the sentence level, therefore, we need to distinguish between helping students learn how to correct their mechanics, punctuation, and grammar and how to make wise choices of style. These tasks call for attention at different times in the writing process and may call for different methods.

The Current State of Student Writing

Why students need continuing study and work on sentences for mechanical errors and also for style demands consideration before we approach the *how* of such study. Many instructors feel emotionally afflicted at the sight of mechanical or grammatical errors in student writing, wonder what to do about them, and because of them may conclude that student writing in general has hopelessly degenerated. *Why, they wonder, must instructors in college still face the job of helping students learn to write correctly?*

But has student writing degenerated? Have high schools failed in their job? Here are four considerations to modify our reactions.

- *Most teachers when reading students' writing are automatically on the lookout for sentence-level errors.* We may scour essays for such errors even before we contemplate what the student is trying to say. Joseph Williams (Emeritus Professor of English at the University of Chicago and author of the classic text *Style: Ten Lessons in Clarity and Grace*) observes in his essay "The Phenomenology of Error" that we search for errors in students' writing with an industry unlike that which we apply to anyone else's work. He makes this point convincingly at the end of his essay when he reveals that it is filled with "errors," few of which, if any, we will have noticed. We look for and find errors where we expect them: in student writing.

- *Sometimes it is actually easier to notice and comment on sentence-level errors than on the more substantive problems of a student's essay.* We may find it daunting to determine how to help the student who shows only a thin knowledge of the essay's topic, who has proposed a thinner thesis, and who has supported it with the thinnest of evidence. It's easier by far to locate the source of our distress in sentence fragments, spelling errors, and improper citation methods, even though we might barely notice these errors if the essay's substance were sound.

- *Some of the "errors" that so greatly alarm us in student writing are not absolute matters of right and wrong but are determined only by taste and discipline — they are actually matters of style.* For example, opinions vary by discipline and occasion about whether or not the use of *I* or of the passive voice is permissible. We also often count as error "rules" which are in fact matters of etiquette in formal standard usage. For instance, the distinction between *that* and *which* — frequently a target for teachers who bemoan students' "bad grammar" — is a rule that, according to Joseph Williams, "first appeared in 1906 in Henry and Francis Fowler's *The King's English.* . . . The Fowlers thought that the random variation between *that* and *which* in restrictive clauses was messy, so they simply asserted that henceforth writers should (with some exceptions) limit *which* to nonrestrictive clauses" (*Style* 24). The "rule" has existed ever since, primarily in the handbooks of grammarians, but rarely in the practice of professional writers, including that of grammarians themselves.

- *Studies show that students aren't, in fact, making more mistakes.* In an extensive study they made in 1988, Robert Connors and Andrea Lunsford found that "college students are *not* making more formal errors in writing than they used to" as compared with students studied in 1917 and 1930, although the errors are different (more spelling errors, for instance). They also found that "teachers' ideas about what constitutes a serious, markable error vary widely. . . . Some teachers pounce on every 'very unique' as a pet peeve, some rail at 'Every student . . . their. . . .' The most prevalent error, failure to place a comma after an introductory word or phrase, was a *bête noire* for some teachers but was ignored by many more" (402). We ourselves confess that we continue compulsively to root out students' misuse of *hopefully,* even knowing that the battle is virtually lost: it is to be hoped that some future generation of teachers will neither know nor care that *hopefully* once meant *only* "full of hope."

The Recursive Nature of Learning to Write

But sometimes we read a student's essay, whether in a first-year or upper-level course, and find that at the sentence level the writing is, beyond question, poor. There may be fractures in the grammar, flawed mechanics, inappropriate choice of style, or shifts in register.

Interested as he was in the production of sentences, Joseph Williams pursued the question of why first-year law students so often write terrible prose, leading their professors to question not just how they got into law school in the first place but how they got such high grades in college. The gist of Williams's insight into the situation is that learning to write is not a linear progression. Getting to a certain degree of excellence in one field is no guarantee of excellence when a person writes in another. Instead, the development of writing skill, like the process of writing, is recursive. When students start to write in a new and difficult subject, they may get into trouble with sentence structure, with use of vocabulary, even with control over basic sentence correctness. Most of those first-year law school students had been fine writers before and would be again. Given enough practice, they would produce correct and even stylistically elegant sentences; eventually they might edit the *Law Review*. Writing effectively was simply a process they had to relearn, even at the sentence level of grammar and style. The same is true, Williams observes, for freshmen in college. They don't need to be immediately belabored about error: they need practice with their subjects (Williams, "On the Maturing," and Williams and Colomb, "The University of Chicago").

It seems, then, that students' essays may not always deserve such intense scrutiny as we may wish to provide from the get-go. When students do have trouble, immediate and primary attention to errors or to stylistic choices may not solve the problem. It is nevertheless true that improvements are often in order. Given the above background, the question is when, where, and how we might provide assistance with error and with style.

When, Where, and How to Attend to Sentences

Let's tackle first what seems to many to be the most aggravating problem, namely, how to help students rid their sentences of errors.

Who Attends to Error, and When?

Few teachers have confronted the problem of error and etiquette — deviation from standard English — more directly than Peter Elbow, who has dedicated his life to teaching writing and to thinking about how best to teach writing. In a recent discussion of the needs of unskilled writers, "especially writers who grew up using nonprestige dialects of English" ("Inviting" 365), Elbow asks how, in one semester, an instructor can avoid crippling students by asking that they constantly attend to error, and yet prepare them to produce standard written English (SWE). We cannot teach students everything they need to know in our individual classrooms, he points out, and if we try to do so, we will focus on just the wrong thing: surface features of language rather than substance. We will also tend to discredit nonacademic dialects. What should we do?

Elbow observes that "correctness" has little to do with *substantive criteria* for judging writing, that is, "the criteria that most teachers use in judging most essays: sticking to the topic or question or assignment; getting the information or concepts right; having good ideas of one's own; reasoning carefully; giving enough arguments, evidence, and examples; organizing effectively; and making meaning clear at the sentence level" (382). He points out that "it is possible to meet every one of those criteria and still use lots of language people call wrong" (382).

So in multiple drafts Elbow allows, indeed encourages, his students to use any dialect, any language, they want. In a final, separate step, however, Elbow requires that the essay be submitted in SWE. And here is the catch: he makes "not the impossible demand that all [his] students know enough about English grammar and conventions of usage to [copyedit] without help, but rather the pragmatic and feasible demand that they know how to take charge of their writing process" (367).

> What Elbow wants is that students acquire "the practical ability to take whatever steps are necessary to get the desired grammar, syntax, punctuation, and spelling — *even if that means getting help*" from "spell checkers, grammar programs . . . , writing centers, learning labs, roommates, friends, loved ones, and even paid typists or editors" (366–67).

The main point, Elbow asserts, is that "as teachers of writing, we need to recognize that taking whatever steps are needed for successful copy-editing is an important and inherent part of *what it means to be a writer*" (367). Certainly, any academic or professional writer relies heavily on copy editors, paid or unpaid.

Following Elbow's suggestion may remove a mind- and hope-killing fixation on surface correctness (rather than on substantive criteria for writing) by turning the process over to the writer, making editing or sentence revision simply a job that, as a last step, has to get done. Student writers must learn how to do that job, no matter what kinds of help they need to elicit. It's part of a writer's work. And if they do that work after the substance of the essay has developed, as Elbow suggests, the help they receive will not compromise their authorship of the work.

What Can Instructors Do to Help Students with Error?

Making the editing project a matter-of-fact, finish-the-job task that appears after the real, intellectual work of writing has already occurred can remove the sense of burden from teachers and students alike. Placing attention on error last, and turning responsibility for it over to students, does not mean, however, that instructors can or should abnegate all responsibility for addressing sentences. You should of course seize appropriate occasions and methods for helping students eliminate error. In the following list we offer suggestions for attending to and reducing error in students' drafts and finished essays.

- *Arrange that students act as proofreaders for each other.* In line with making students responsible for their own proofreading, students can proofread one another's completed essays in class before they turn them in. You can use this time to move through the classroom, answer questions, and spot-check the kinds of "errors" they are finding. It's a good idea to have the student editors sign their names to the essays, make suggestions and corrections in pencil, and discuss their proposed changes with the writers. Note that it's best *not* to give students this proofreading task on early drafts when as readers they should be attending critically to substance, not to surface.

- *Encourage listening and reading aloud.* When students proofread their essays, they usually *look* for problems, and if they are just visually scanning the text, they won't find many. Experienced, professional writers, by contrast, usually read aloud or silently vocalize their work while they read. Almost all writers can hear errors, ambiguities, and awkward phrasing before they see those problems.

  Even when they understand why instructors recommend that they read drafts aloud and listen to the language they have used, our students typically ignore this advice in practice, because of habits and time constraints. To reinforce this advice, you can demonstrate its value in class or in conferences. (In conferences we often make a copy of the student paper and read it aloud while the student looks and listens for sentences that need revision.) Helping the writer hear problems is more effective than simply pointing them out or making corrections.

- *Assign a handbook.* While helping students assume responsibility for correctness, you can make sure they know about the resources available to them for assistance. One important resource is the handbook, or writer's reference, which students can read and use for instructions on how to cite Web sources, format the layout of a manuscript, and so on. Students do, however, have to be taught where to find those instructions and be made aware that you insist they follow them. If you know students own a handbook, you can refer them to it for issues of correctness and style.

- *Categorize errors.* When you respond to essays at the editing stage, it's a good idea to focus on the two or three most immediately important sentence-level issues, finding categories into which to group your most common observations. To help a student grasp and correct those problems, you can indicate the presence of a category of error in the essay and include an end comment suggesting ways to solve the problem. You might ask the student to consult a handbook and do a few extra exercises for a particular problem; or you might ask the student to resubmit the essay with a certain category of error corrected. When new essays come in, you can note whether the old errors have or have not disappeared.

- *Have students respond to your responses — an imperative step.* Some years after one of the authors graduated from college, she reviewed the many essays she had written for one of her courses. To her surprise she found that in every essay she had misspelled the same word. An industrious student, she had never paid the least attention to her instructor's correction of her error. If she had had to resubmit the essay to her instructors with all sentence-level errors corrected, she would have been forced to notice the recurring comments. Comments on sentences will do very little good if students don't read and follow up on them — a common situation.

- *Ask students to resubmit edited essays.* It makes sense to ensure that students edit their essays, just as professional writers do after a manuscript has been accepted for publication. At this point students will be working not on ideas or organization but on improving and correcting sentences and on the mechanics of their essays. One way to handle this step is to record a grade for an essay only after the student resubmits it with such matters attended to.

  It can be quite effective to ask students to spend ten minutes in class going over the essays you have just returned and making any required sentence-level corrections or changes. This exercise provides an opportunity to see whether or not they can make the requested changes, and it ensures that students read your comments.

  If it is not possible to have students resubmit essays in polished form, it becomes that much more important to categorize the problems for students, record them in your own records, and attend to those particular features in the students' next writing.

- *Have students review the comments on a set of essays.* A similar technique asks that students periodically review their writing, with your comments, and write a brief report summarizing your observations and explaining how they intend to take action on any difficulties you have been targeting. This procedure ensures that students will review and reflect on your discussion of their work, with some hope that they will apply their insights to future writing.

- *Respond to patterns of sentence-level errors in a set of essays in a subsequent class.* When you are going through a batch of students' essays, one of the simplest ways to attend to sentence-level errors is to notice what mistakes appear in most of them and to start making an exercise sheet for use in class. If, for instance, you notice that many students are having trouble making pronouns and antecedents agree or that they use commas where semicolons or colons are required, you can write down interesting sentences from the essays in which these errors occur.

  An important note: When it is possible (and it isn't always), avoid concentrating only on "correcting" errors. Students often learn more when they practice doing something correctly from the start, rather than going on error hunts; and, of course, this is a much more positive approach to the study of language. For instance, an effective exercise asks students to provide the punctuation for sentences (from student essays or an assigned reading) from which all the punctuation has been omitted.

Who Attends to Style, and When?

Much of the time, sentences that instructors don't care for are actually "correct." The problems lie rather in students' choices of sentence form and of diction. Perhaps the student chose to use the active voice where the passive voice is preferred for most of a lab write-up. Perhaps the student chose a level of diction inappropriate to the situation at hand. Perhaps a student wrote mostly in simple sentences where complex sentences would help create a more sophisticated voice and also would help clarify relationships among ideas.

Many students, however, simply aren't aware of the choices available to them in terms of syntax (including punctuation) and diction and are even less aware that context (genre, discipline, audience) should determine their choices of diction and sentence form. There are some fairly simple methods instructors can use to help students raise their stylistic awareness.

What Can Instructors Do to Help Students Control Stylistic Choices?

- *Have students examine models and imitate them.* Students often think there is just one right way to write. They may have no notion that what is "right" in one place is "wrong" in another. They may expect, indeed want to insist, that you teach them *the* right way to write. You can't do this, but you can spend some time helping students learn that they must always make stylistic *choices*. Indeed, you may want to insist that your students learn how to choose the stylistic characteristics appropriate for your discipline.

  It is therefore helpful to have students examine the different ways in which writers write, because they have different voices or because the occasion or purpose, the genre or discipline, varies. By looking at professional models, you and your students can discuss characteristics of style — of syntax, register, or punctuation — the choices authors make to affect meaning, voice, and tone.

  For instance, students might look at a journal such as the scholarly publication *Science,* where they could compare a research article with its abstract (article: ". . . the seasonal behavior of CO_2 frost at the Martian poles is not symmetric"; abstract: ". . . frost remains at the South Pole of Mars during much or all of the year but disappears during summer at the North Pole" [Paige 1160, 1138]). The language of the article proper is in a more formal register: the sentence is written in a style in which nouns dominate and uses a scientific vocabulary. For the abstract, the authors chose to use stronger verbs and less formal language.

  It can be profitable to spend several minutes in a class comparing paragraphs written by different authors in readings that you have assigned. If you prefer one style to another, make clear why, provide a model, and *have students write short imitations.*

Joseph Williams suggests that students might study and then imitate a sentence that uses multiple coordinated structures, such as this sentence written by Eva Hoffman in "Minor Art Offers Special Pleasures": "For the amateur spectator, such . . . works are the daily fare which provide good, honest nourishment — and which can lead to appreciation of more refined, or deeper pleasures" (Williams, *Style* 180). The relative clauses *which provide good, honest nourishment* and *which can lead to appreciation of more refined, or deeper pleasures* are parallel: *which can lead* parallels *which provide; pleasures* parallels *nourishment;* and *refined, or deeper* parallels *good, honest.* Students can experiment with sentences that construct similar parallel clauses.

Students can try to re-create a writer's style. It can be very effective to type a short passage from an admired writer, minus the punctuation, and have the students then supply the punctuation, eventually checking their choices against the author's. Or you can make all the sentences short. Students then combine sentences, using subordination or coordination. If instead you have combined sentences, students can try to shorten them.

- *Provide models from students' essays.* Often you can turn to students' essays for sentences that provide excellent models of choices in syntax and diction. You can use these in class for discussion and for later imitation. Perhaps you might cull well-written sentences that illustrate features you'd like to promote and have students imitate — perhaps a sentence that lays out a clear three-part parallel structure, perhaps several sentences that beautifully incorporate a quotation, perhaps a sentence that (like this one) employs *anaphora*, the repetition of an opening word for a sequence of clauses or sentences.

- *Assign mini-essays for practice.* It's one thing to read instructions and analyze someone else's style and another to put observation into practice. Have students write a paragraph in which they quote and discuss a source, or in which they imitate a particular style (short sentences or long; differing levels of formality), or in which they choose between a colon or a dash for the preferred construction of voice. Review these sample paragraphs and have students compare their creations with professional models.

- *Encourage listening and reading aloud.* When we read aloud, as anyone who has given a speech knows, we catch the infelicities of sentence structure and use of diction that may have eluded us when we read our text silently. Our ears catch the fact that every sentence ends with the same word; we notice when a sentence structure lacks grace.

- *Assign essays with varying rhetorical contexts* (see Chapter 2). Students of animal science might write two reports on why a cat died, one intended for the files, the other for an audience of doctors. They then can report the same case in a letter addressed to the owners of the cat. Students can write grant proposals, letters to senators, memos — all selected by the instructor according to the genre typically used in a subject, all requiring that the student control different styles, make deliberate choices about diction and sentence syntax.

- *Ask students to include certain kinds of sentences in their essays and to underline the sentences so that you can identify them quickly.* Requiring students to incorporate a colon, for instance, can result immediately in more sophisticated choices of syntax. (See the section "Sentence Patterns Worth Discussing" later in this chapter for other possible candidates.)

- *Collect sentences from a batch of student writing that could benefit from stylistic improvement.* If, for instance, you notice sentences with missed opportunities for coordination or parallelism, or sentences that rely on the passive voice where the active would be preferable, you can collect those for use in in-class workshops.

- *Have students analyze their own styles.* Students can study their own style by choosing one or two paragraphs in an essay they have written and circling all the subjects or all the verbs, counting the length of each sentence, or examining their use of parallelism, coordination, or subordination (see discussion of these terms later in this chapter).

Aspects of Error and Style Meriting Attention

Some readers may be thinking that it is all very well to talk about how to respond to sentence-level issues but that it's difficult to do so if as the instructor you don't know what to say about sentences.

You see a sentence and know something is wrong but can't figure out what. You'd like to talk about style, but you have never studied it. It is tempting at this point to say that because you are an educated person, you know enough already to be able to talk to students about their writing, even at the sentence level. You make sentence-level decisions all the time. Anything you don't notice is probably not worth noticing. To an extent, this is true. It is also true that it is wise to teach only what you know very well and are confident about.

> Acting on a little half-learned, superficially acquired knowledge about sentences can be more harmful than doing nothing: it is worse to "correct" a student for an error that doesn't exist than to say nothing at all when you are in doubt.

For instance, we have observed that instructors may, in an excess of semi-informed zeal, call any verb form that includes is (*She is going to the store now*) a "passive" verb and therefore request changes.

So a bit of selective, though thorough, study can be a very good thing. As we have already mentioned, when you decide to engage in sentence-level instruction, in whatever form and however minimal, you can end up confusing students rather than helping them if you haven't straightened out your own understanding of the basic vocabulary of sentences. Fortunately, as an educated person who writes a great deal, you have much intuitive knowledge that can quickly become conscious knowledge. Conscious knowledge can make it considerably easier to assist students who have produced what could otherwise seem to be just peculiarly awkward sentences.

This book, however, is not the place in which to provide a course in sentence analysis. Like the authors, you may find it interesting and gratifying to consult a handbook or a book on style, even if you don't assign one to your students.

Two excellent texts are Joseph Williams's *Style: Ten Lessons in Clarity and Grace* and Richard Lanham's *Revising Prose*. These are not handbooks, which are sources of rules and other general information about writing. Rather, they describe how sentences work; both tackle this project primarily in terms of subjects and verbs. Both are extremely smart books that can be used for the analysis of prose in almost any field. John Trimble's *Writing with Style: Conversations on the Art of Writing* also provides an excellent introduction to the subject.

Having said that we cannot here provide you with a course on sentence analysis, we can, however, provide you with a list of the twenty most common errors in student writing as well as a quick rundown of "things to look for" in sentences that will help with the study of style. If the terms we use here — or the rules of correctness — are not familiar to you, you will probably want to do a bit of brushing up by consulting a writer's reference. (A good and very popular example is Diana Hacker's *A Writer's Reference*.)

The Twenty Most Common Errors

According to Connors and Lunsford's extensive 1988 study, the twenty errors occurring most commonly in student essays are as follows, in descending order of frequency (403). We have supplied short examples for some errors and discuss others in the paragraphs that follow.

1. No comma after introductory element [*Well it wasn't really true.*]

2. Vague pronoun reference [*See discussion below.*]

3. No comma in compound sentence [*I like to eat but I hate to gain weight.*]

4. Wrong word [*His F in math enhanced his alarm about his D in chem.*]

5. No comma with nonrestrictive element [*See discussion below.*]

6. Wrong or missing inflected verb endings [*I use to go often to town.*]

7. Wrong or missing preposition [*Moosewood Restaurant is located at Ithaca.*]

8. Comma splice [*See discussion below.*]

9. Possessive apostrophe [*Student's backpacks weigh far too much.*]

10. Tense shift [*I was happily watching TV when suddenly my sister attacks me.*]

11. Unnecessary shift in person (pronoun) [*When one is tired, you should sleep.*]

12. Sentence fragment [*See discussion below.*]

13. Wrong tense or verb form [*I would not have said that if I thought it would have shocked her.*]

14. Subject-verb agreement [*Having many close friends, especially if you've known them for a long time, are a great help in times of trouble.*]

15. Lack of comma in a series [*Students eat, sleep and do homework.*]

16. Pronoun agreement [*See discussion below.*]

17. Unnecessary comma(s) with restrictive element [*The novel, that my teacher assigned, was very boring.*]

18. Run-on or fused sentence [*He loved the seminar he even loved the readings.*]

19. Dangling or misplaced modifier [*After being put to sleep, a small incision is made below the navel.*]

20. Its/it's error [*Its a splendid day for everyone.*]

These are errors you may spend some time on, whether with individual students or in class. Notice that many of these mistakes have to do with punctuation, primarily with the proper use of the comma. The following are explanations of a few of the less self-explanatory errors. (For more complete information, consult Lunsford, *The St. Martin's Handbook* 13–27. Lunsford offers explanations and examples to accompany the "twenty most common errors" list.)

Number 2, Vague pronoun reference. John told his father that his car had been stolen. The reader cannot know whether the second *his* refers to John or to John's father.

Number 5, No comma(s) with nonrestrictive element. A nonrestrictive element contains information that could be omitted. It therefore requires a comma (or commas) to set it off from the word it describes.

When the comma or commas are omitted, the meaning can be changed to something quite different from what was intended. In the following example (b) alters the meaning of (a). (a) *The students, who had unsuccessfully concealed their participation in the prank, were expelled.* (b) *The students who had unsuccessfully concealed their participation in the prank were expelled.* Sentence (b), without commas, distinguishes between what happened to students who didn't conceal their guilt and those who did. Sentence (a), with commas, simply adds information about the students.

Number 8, Comma splices. Comma splices use commas, without a conjunction, to join two or more clauses that can stand alone grammatically; they are the cause of the most common form of run-on sentence in student writing. Writers use a comma as a stop, where they should have used a period or a semicolon. These punctuation errors often occur when novice writers mistake conjunctive adverbs such as *however* or *therefore* for conjunctions. Instead of writing *Chloe liked the cat; however, she was allergic to it,* they will write *Chloe liked the cat, however, she was allergic to it.*

Number 12, Sentence fragment. Sentence fragments usually occur when writers fail to attach a phrase with a comma to the preceding sentence, *not* because the fragment needs a subject and verb. (*He went shopping in the local sports store. An outing he usually enjoyed* becomes, correctly, *He went shopping in the local sports store, an outing he usually enjoyed.*)

Number 16, Pronoun agreement error. When someone plagiarizes from material on a Web site, they are likely to be caught. Someone is singular, but the pronoun *they* is plural. The sentence can be revised in several ways: *When someone plagiarizes from material on a Web site, he or she is likely to be caught.* Or *When students plagiarize from a Web site, they are likely to be caught.*

Sentence Patterns Worth Discussing for Style

You will probably find it more interesting and productive to help students investigate such matters as style or register (rather than errors per se), because in these areas students learn that they must make choices rather than just follow rules and that these choices give them control over their writing, over their voices. Both Joseph Williams and Richard Lanham emphasize the subject (or agent) and verb (the action) as the basis of clear, controlled sentence construction. You can often help students write better sentences by examining the following features of their sentences.

THE SUBJECTS OF SENTENCES

- Are the subjects/topics of the sentence made the agents of the action (subjects of clauses)? *It is impossible for your claims to be proved conclusively* vs. *Your claims cannot be proved conclusively* (Williams, *Style* 106).

- *Are sentence subjects used consistently throughout a passage of text?*

Inconsistent subjects:

The patient is 5'4" and weighs about 84 lb. A *high-calorie diet* will help her gain weight. Constipation will be controlled by a high-fiber diet.

Consistent subjects:

The patient is 5'4" and weighs about 84 lb. A *high-calorie diet* will help her gain weight. A *high-fiber diet* will control her constipation.

The *patient* is 5'4" and weighs about 84 lb. To gain weight *she* should go on a high-calorie diet. To control her constipation, *she* should maintain a high-fiber diet.

THE VERBS

- Does the student rely on forms of *to be* (is, was, are, etc.)? (*I am hoping that I will be getting an A in the course* vs. *I hope that I get an A in the course. He was angry* vs *He reacted angrily.*)

- Does the student put action into noun or verb form? (*His* reaction *to the speech was an angry one* vs. *He* reacted *angrily to the speech.*)

- Does the student have control over the choice between active and passive voice? (*Decisions to plagiarize were made widely across campus* vs. *Many students across campus decided to plagiarize.*)

PREPOSITIONAL PHRASES

- Does the writer string together long sequences of prepositional phrases? (*Throughout our lives, we are exposed to a lot of different teachings and one of them, in our society, is the value placed upon a life in which we are successful* vs. *Our society teaches the value of success* (Lanham 49, 50).

SUBORDINATION, COORDINATION, PARALLELISM

- Does the writer have control of a range of options? Can she or he decide among the following possibilities?

(a) I committed my sin in haste; I repented my sin at leisure.

(b) I committed my sin in haste, and I repented my sin at leisure.

(c) Although I committed my sin in haste, I repented my sin at leisure.

In sentence (a) the writer relies on *parallel structure* to connect the two sentences (and two ideas): the two parts of the sentence are identical in structure (subject, verb, direct object, adverbial preposi- tional phrase; certain words are repeated in the same spots).

Sentence (b) *coordinates* the two clauses with a coordinating con- junction, *and.*

As in sentence (b), some novice writers rely on *and* where *subordi- nation,* as in sentence (c), would be used more suitably to reveal cause and effect, to establish hierarchies. Subordination is created by the use of *although,* to construct a *subordinate clause.*

SENTENCE LENGTH

- Does the writer appropriately vary the lengths of sentences? Some students write sentences that are all about twelve to fifteen words long. They may not know how to construct a longer sentence, or they think that long sentences are "bad." They may also not appreciate the rhetorical force of a very short sentence.

- Does the writer vary the parts of speech at the beginnings of sentences? Sentences consistently beginning *Orwell says* or *This is / There is* may indicate that the writer is summarizing rather than analyzing. Students' lack of sophistication in sentence structure may be revealed by their beginning most sentences directly with the subject rather than with a prepositional phrase, a participle, or (especially) with a subordinate clause. Such students often begin sentences with *This is* or *There is* because they do not connect sentences to each other with the use of introductory elements.

Example:

Orwell considers the use of the passive voice to be politically significant. *He* believes this because he sees that politicians use the passive voice to conceal their misdeeds. *He* thinks that the passive voice even helps them to conceal their misdeeds from themselves.

Rewrite:

Orwell considers the use of the passive voice to be politically significant. *Observing* that politicians use the passive voice to conceal their misdeeds, he accuses them of concealing their misdeeds even from themselves.

COLONS AND SEMICOLONS TO CREATE CONNECTIONS

- Our experience suggests that many beginning writers, fearing error, systematically avoid using colons and semicolons alto- gether. A student who can control colons can produce the follow- ing sentence, with its more sophisticated connection of ideas, rather than the sentence in the preceding example.

Orwell considers the use of the passive voice to be politically significant: observing that politicians use the passive voice to conceal their mis-

deeds, he accuses them of concealing their misdeeds even from themselves.

For a much more thorough discussion of how to analyze sentences,
consult a book such as those by Williams and Lanham. Any writer's
reference will provide helpful information and examples on such matters as subordination, coordination, and parallelism, areas in which
students can often benefit from developmental exercises.

Responding to the Sentence-Level Problems of ESL Students

Students for whom English is a second language (ESL students) may
make sentence-level errors and have difficulties that differ from those
of native speakers. You may therefore want to respond somewhat differently to the essays of ESL students and provide different kinds of
assistance. As with native speakers, you may find, however, that the
response to your assistance is slower than you would wish. Learning
takes time, usually more than you will get to spend with these students. From our colleague Judith Pierpont, a specialist in helping ESL
students with their writing, we have learned the value of the following
practices.

- *Provide additional time and practice.* For the most part, nonnative speakers of English will benefit from the same kinds of
  assistance that you provide native speakers. Nonnative speakers
  may, however, need extended deadlines, additional drafts, and
  more opportunities to edit. You may have to decide whether you
  want to see only correct work from ESL students, with an accom-
  panying decrease in richness of thought, or if you want to encourage depth of thought and elicit correctness later.

- *Discuss the most appropriate kinds of response to students' essays.*
  When responding to the writing of ESL students, it can be
  helpful to consult with students about what type of response, in
  terms of sentence correctness, they consider to be most helpful.
  Do they need to have you actually make the changes (for example, insert or delete articles in the writing of Asian language
  speakers)? Do they prefer that you underline errors so they can
  figure out what's wrong on their own? Do they require only that
  you put an X in the margin, leaving the search for the error up to
  them?
    Your ESL students will be at different stages of expertise,
  and the method should be chosen to suit their abilities. Many
  ESL student writers will know the "rules" better than you do, but
  (as with native speakers) you can help them by identifying
  patterns of error and then giving them opportunities to make the
  needed corrections and practice correct patterns.

We might note that, even more than with native speakers, it would be unfair to judge the worth of an essay in terms only, or primarily, of its sentence correctness. Let ESL student writers know — and demonstrate to them — that you are interested in *what* they have to say, not just (at the sentence level) *how* they say it.

- *Help ESL students learn how to take charge of correctness on their own.* As with native speakers, you can encourage ESL students to take charge of correctness on their own, by any devices available to them, whether those include getting able roommates, friends, or members of their families to review the final drafts or consulting tutors at your institution's writing center. You can certainly encourage ESL students to take advantage of the tutorial service offered by your school. If you are actively working with these students on ESL issues, however, make sure that they tell you the kinds of assistance they have received, and when you want to know what they can do on their own, tell them not to get help from others.

- *Seek outside assistance.* Many colleges and universities employ one or more specialists in the teaching of ESL students. If you find that you have a number of such students in your classes, you might benefit from consulting with these specialists to make sure that you are neither shortchanging your students nor overburdening yourself with unneeded or unhelpful efforts. Some institutions are able to provide additional assistance for ESL students beyond what you can give.

Do not be surprised if you fail to eradicate all error from your students' writing or to transform their writing styles: getting rid of old habits may not happen in the semester that students spend with you, no matter how insistent you are, but other teachers may reap the fruits of your instruction. And also, do you recall all those mistakes and infelicities you've found in your own supposedly thoroughly proofed manuscripts?

7

Orchestrating the Research Paper

Key Elements

The Research Paper: Differing Conceptions and Goals   105

Common features in research papers include a longer length and use of documented, multiple sources of information. Because disciplines differ in their requirements, if you assign a research paper you will need to specify (1) the kind of writing you have in mind, including its form and purpose, (2) the intended audience, and (3) the kinds of sources you expect students to use.

Disappointment with research papers persists largely because students' misconceptions of investigative writing remain unacknowledged and therefore unresolved. Problems inherent in the linear student research method mean that undergraduates in a field of study are not in a position to produce works of authoritative scholarship in that field without extensive guidance from their teachers.

Effective Guidance for Students' Research Projects   110

Assign research papers in stages, with guidance from you or from other students at each stage:

- A brief proposal
- An introductory portion of a draft
- A full draft of the paper
- Class presentations
- Submission of the finished paper

Some strategies to employ in written comments on works in progress, conferences, and material you distribute to the class:

- Help students convert topics into questions or positions.
- Recommend good sources and research strategies.
- Recommend dialectical notes.
- Specify a system of documentation.
- Comment most extensively on proposals and drafts.
- Provide models for the types of writing you expect.

Creating Opportunities for Presentation and Exchange   117

As renditions of scholarship, investigative projects will be more meaningful if student writers also have an audience of peers, in addition to their teacher. Opportunities might include peer reviews, brief presentations, and group presentations.

Advice for Preventing Plagiarism   118

Types and causes of plagiarism — two extremes:

- Conscious deception to gain unfair advantage over other students
- Plagiarism that results from confusion and brings neither significant advantage to the writer nor disadvantage to others

Many students drift into minor forms of plagiarism because the approach they have used does not give them a sense of position from which they can easily distinguish their ideas and voices from those of other writers. Most of the strategies we have recommended for orchestrating the research paper are also strategies for preventing plagiarism of all kinds. Make sure your students are aware of the risks involved in deceptive plagiarism and link the topics for research papers closely to the content of your course.

The Research Paper: Differing Conceptions and Goals

College teachers and their students talk about research papers (or "term papers") as though they were referring to a single form of writing, consistent across disciplines and levels of instruction. Teachers often assign research papers at the beginning of the term and collect the finished products at the end, with the assumption that undergraduates have learned how to produce this kind of writing in high school or in freshman writing classes. And most college students do seem to have fixed conceptions of a research paper, along with methods for writing one. "I have three research papers due next week," students say, referring to assignments in different courses as a common type of writing.

But what is a research paper, exactly? Is it a specific form of writing, like a literary theme paper or a lab report? When they assign and produce research papers, do college teachers and their students have the same kind of writing in mind?

We should consider these basic questions before we propose methods for guiding students through research writing projects.

Common Features

Research papers do have some very general features in common:

- Ranging from seven or eight to more than thirty pages, they are typically longer than other writing assignments in college courses and carry more weight in the final grade.

- The term *research* distinguishes such papers from other writing because students are supposed to investigate the topic and locate sources with some degree of independent initiative. Research papers also involve references to multiple sources of information and thus require a system for acknowledging and distinguishing these sources, with citations in the text and a bibliography at the end.

The Research Paper in Different Disciplines,
Courses, and Levels of Instruction

Within the very broad parameters of the common features just discussed, research papers vary almost as much as other writing assignments do, depending on the discipline, the level of instruction, and the specific goals of the course and instructor.

Like other assigned writing, a research paper might take the form of an objective report, an explanation, a topical summary, an argument, an interpretation of a text, or analysis of an issue. Depending on these forms and purposes, the discipline, and the course level, relevant sources vary as well. A history paper, for example, might require analysis of primary documents such as diaries, newspaper articles, or public records from a specific period. A literature paper might develop an interpretation of a novel with reference to secondary sources in criticism, theory, and biography. Scientific papers at advanced levels are often based entirely on professional research articles, while students at lower levels of the science curriculum use sources written for general audiences.

Because varying disciplines differ in their requirements, if you assign a research paper you will therefore need to specify (1) the kind of writing you have in mind, including its form and purpose; (2) the intended audience; and (3) the kinds of sources you expect students to use.

Even if your students have completed research papers in high school, in freshman composition, or in other college courses, this experience will not provide reliable models for the specific type of research paper you want them to produce.

Differences Between Students' and Teachers' Goals and Conceptions

While the research paper is not a clearly defined genre of writing, college teachers do have fairly consistent reasons for assigning these projects. Their goals are often at odds, however, with the objectives and methods with which undergraduates approach investigative writing. If you understand the basic differences, you can help your students adapt not only to your expectations but also to those of other college teachers. Disappointment with this kind of student writing persists largely because students' misconceptions of investigative writing remain unacknowledged and therefore unresolved.

Many of us remember research papers as the most valuable learning experiences in our undergraduate studies — even as the incentives for graduate work and careers in our fields. These projects were important turning points because they gave us a taste of real scholarship: the opportunity to pursue a line of inquiry on our own and to write about our discoveries with a real sense of authority over the subject.

This is the kind of experience college teachers want to offer their students when they assign research papers. They know that independent inquiry can encourage types of learning students will not acquire through lectures, required readings, and other conventional methods of instruction.

When they assign research projects, teachers hope to give undergraduates

- an experience of real investigative scholarship in the discipline

- a sense of authority over a specific topic in the course

- practice identifying and pursuing a significant question

- experience synthesizing material from a variety of sources

- exposure to professional literature in the field

- practice using library resources, research methods, and systems of documentation

In most cases, however, we produced our own memorable research papers toward the end of our undergraduate studies, when we had already developed strong interests in a field of study. Students who have not developed such interests and background knowledge will tend to approach a research paper as a routine academic exercise: a test of their ability to gather, report on, and document information on an unfamiliar topic. This is typically the purpose of research papers assigned in high schools.

Because they view research papers as information-gathering exercises, undergraduates routinely approach the task with a linear series of procedures:

- Choose a topic.

- Locate some sources on the topic.

- Read the source material, taking notes and recording quotations on note cards.

- Construct an outline from the note cards.

- Following the outline, write sections of the paper, incorporating source material in appropriate sections.

- Document references and proofread.

- Turn it in.

These and related procedures will get research papers completed fairly efficiently, but they rarely produce the kinds of investigative writing teachers hope to read. Such methods do *not* include occasions for

- narrowing the focus of the research

- identifying significant questions

- selecting references most relevant to those questions

- thinking about the research material

- developing a position and voice as a real author

When students who follow the typical procedures reach the writing stage, they tend to write about whatever happens to be recorded on their note cards, drawn from sources they located before they knew much about the topic. At that stage, substantial refocusing and revision would require further research with new sources, and much of the material they initially collected would become irrelevant. When they have already become invested in the material at hand, and when the clock is ticking toward the deadline, they will usually ignore second thoughts and write about the information they have gathered, more or less at random, in their notes.

Problems with the Linear Student Research Method

Ending at the beginning. Papers written directly from research notes usually look like drafts: preparations for writing a *real* research paper. Because writers who are unfamiliar with the subject cannot begin with a frame of reference that allows them to identify a significant question, the process of research and writing becomes a process of building a frame of reference. And this is why really interesting questions or arguments are often buried in categorized sections or emerge only in the conclusion. As one professor observed, "They want to tell you what the territory looked like as they walked over it." Undergraduate research papers typically end, therefore, where real works of scholarship begin.

Losing the author. These linear methods also subordinate the author of the paper to the authors of source material, and in extreme cases the student research paper does not really have an author. Instead, the role of the writer is simply that of putting together the knowledge and ideas of real authorities — real authors — on the subject. When student writers have not developed a sense of authority, position, and voice in relation to the subject, they have difficulty figuring out how to include and acknowledge the voices and perspectives of other writers.

Inability to distinguish common knowledge from other new information. The rule of thumb most students have learned for the purpose of deciding how to acknowledge sources is that they should cite all information and ideas they got from others, unless the information is common knowledge. For writers who knew little about the subject when they began the project, however, this rule poses a dilemma. All of the information in the paper comes from other sources, and when they know nothing about the subject to begin with, it is difficult to define "common knowledge." Common to whom? To the general public? To experts on this subject? Clear answers to these questions depend on a sharply defined sense of position, context, and audience that novice writers do not have. As a consequence, undergraduate research papers tend to err in one direction or the other: either to cite almost everything or to appropriate source material in long passages of uncited paraphrase. The latter approach leads writers into certain kinds of plagiarism, which we will discuss at the end of this chapter.

When student writers are left entirely to their own devices, therefore, few of them will produce research papers that fulfill the goals with which teachers assigned these projects. Responsibility for the common flaws we have described does not belong to high school and freshman writing instructors. Instead, we need to recognize that novices in a field of study are not in a position to produce works of authoritative scholarship in that field without extensive guidance from the teachers who assign investigative projects in their courses.

No one but the teachers who require research papers can provide the necessary guidance. High school teachers, for example, cannot show students how to identify significant questions, find appropriate sources, and develop a sense of authority in specialized fields of college study. And only the adept and highly motivated students can accomplish these feats on their own, without help from their teachers.

Effective Guidance for Students' Research Projects

Misgivings about Research Papers

When students produce research papers without guidance in the process, the results are often so disappointing that teachers abandon these assignments, with the bleak conclusion that their students are simply incapable of doing this kind of writing well. We also know professors who, without blaming students or former teachers, have concluded that the research paper itself is a misbegotten form of writing that we cannot reasonably expect undergraduates to produce, except perhaps in the most advanced courses. In some fields, furthermore, the types of research papers described in writing textbooks and assigned in writing classes do not correspond with any form of professional writing and seem to have neither models nor purposes in the discipline.

Recognizing the potential value of research projects, teachers in large classes often convince themselves that their students will reap benefits on their own without supervision or believe, as one professor wryly observed, "that there is value in the Frankenstein work of synthesis, even if it creates little monsters." For most students, however, the benefits of unsupervised research projects will be limited to the challenges of locating sources on a topic and assembling that material in a patchwork of references. These and other goals can be accomplished more effectively with smaller and more narrowly defined assignments. If you want your students to locate, read, and report on professional articles in your field, for example, you can ask them to discuss two or three current articles on a specific topic in a five-page paper.

> Considering common misgivings about research papers and the experiences that inform them, we therefore do not encourage you to assign research papers without providing guidance to students in various stages of the process. We must also acknowledge that providing this guidance requires more time than you are likely to have available in large courses, unless you have teaching assistants or other support staff to help you.

Providing Adequate Guidance

If you do choose to assign longer research papers with several references, we strongly encourage you to assign stages in the process of developing these papers, with guidance from you or from other students at each stage. While these projects are most rewarding to students in advanced courses in their major or minor concentrations, with adequate supervision college freshmen and sophomores can also produce appropriately focused, cohesive research papers based on excellent sources. We have found that the collective quality of this work is directly correlated with the amount of guidance students receive in the process.

Depending on the level of your course, the backgrounds of your students, the complexity of the project, and your goals, the stages of work you assign can vary, but these are some of the most useful elements of staged assignments:

- A *brief proposal* (one or two pages) that describes the focus or research question, with a list of initial sources (sometimes annotated).

- An *introductory portion of a draft* (perhaps three or four pages) with an explanation or outline of following sections and notes on particular questions or problems the writer has encountered.

- A *full draft of the paper*, with citations and bibliography, for your feedback and/or peer review.

- *Class presentations* on these projects, by individuals or small groups.

- *Submission of the finished paper.*

DUE DATES   For obvious reasons, due dates for this work in progress should be evenly distributed throughout the weeks designated for the project, and the proposal with initial sources should be in your hands as early as possible. Because procrastination has especially damning effects on this kind of writing, appropriately spaced stages can greatly improve the quality of the papers simply by structuring time for thoughtful development. If you hope to see substantial revisions, furthermore, you will need to receive drafts at least three weeks before the end of the term, to leave time for feedback, revision, and return of the finished papers. Teachers frequently leave too little time at the end of the process, and find themselves with sad piles of uncollected research papers when the term is over.

THE PROPOSAL   Of all the stages we listed, the proposal with initial sources is probably most crucial to the success of investigative projects; and if we were limited to one occasion for offering guidance in the process, this is the one we would choose. Because novice writers do not yet have a frame of reference for identifying research questions and positions when they begin their projects, their initial "topic" is almost invariably too broad and unfocused. Without advice at this stage, most of them will go on to write about the topic as initially conceived. For the same reasons, initial sources that students locate will be of mixed quality and relevance to a focused treatment of the subject, yet without help they will probably not find better references. While guidance at the proposal stage will not guarantee good papers in the end, lack of guidance can guarantee bad ones.

NO PREPARATORY OUTLINE   Many teachers will find it odd that we do not include an outline stage — one of the most commonly assigned steps in the development of research papers. One reason is that outlines have particularly uneven value. Some writers find them useful, and a roughly equal proportion does not. At the early stages of complex projects, furthermore, outlines tend to lock student writers into premature, categorical approaches to the subject, based on the material and ideas they initially have on hand. And these categorical outlines can create *appearances* of order and cohesion that will dissolve in the writing, in ways that are difficult to predict from the outline itself.

If we want the writer's approach to remain flexible and exploratory, therefore, brief proposals and initial portions of drafts are more useful and revealing as a basis for feedback. Outlines of unfinished portions, however, can give you a clearer sense of the direction the work might take from a fully articulated point of departure.

THE BENEFITS OF CONFERENCES   In small classes, many teachers prefer to hold individual conferences with their students, especially to discuss proposals and references but also to plan the revision of drafts. A half-hour conference can be not only an effective way to sort out complex issues but also an efficient one, given the time required to write useful comments on work in progress. Some kinds of general advice can also be delivered to the entire class, either in spoken comments or in a handout.

The following suggestions may apply to written comments on work in progress, to conferences, or to material you distribute to the class:

- *Help Students to Convert Topics into Questions or Positions*

  When undergraduates choose topics for research, in most cases they do not yet have specific questions, viewpoints, or positions necessary to bring their research and writing into focus. Their initial topics simply define areas of subject matter: the Monroe Doctrine, sexual selection, sleep cycles, the United Auto Workers, special relativity, butterfly migration. Hundreds of research papers, based on specific questions or positions, could be written about each of these topics, and for each of them thousands of references are available.

  When students propose to write on general topics, rather than about specific questions or positions, the most basic question you need to ask is *Why are you writing?* Until they identify particular questions or issues that motivate their research, they will not be able to write from focused viewpoints, in voices of their own. If you then give them examples of appropriately focused questions within the subject area, they can recognize the kind of position they need to reach. This help is especially important because many students believe that once they have chosen a topic the first step in the process is complete. Instead, they need to develop and refine their position continually while they complete research and write a draft.

- *Recommend Good Sources and Research Strategies*

   On their own, many students will find sources on their topics through general subject searches in library indexes and on the Internet. When they have collected a sufficient number of references, they will end that stage of the process and begin to read, while taking notes. But these research methods yield an uneven collection of references at best, with many sources out of date or of marginal quality, especially on the Internet.

   Instead, they need to begin by locating a couple of recent, authoritative sources that contain bibliographical references to others, usually of similar quality. In some cases assigned texts for the course can provide these points of departure into networks of good references. If the texts do not, you should suggest some promising books, articles, or journals to get the process started. In any case, you should recommend these strategies or others as alternatives to the "grab bag" approach.

- *Recommend Dialectical Notes*

   If students use note cards (or notebooks) only to record information they find in references, when they begin to write they will not have voices or viewpoints of their own, and the resulting papers will often look like patchworks of quotation and paraphrase. Clever writers can develop a sense of position while they compose drafts, but ideally this development should occur during their research.

   For this purpose students should take separate notes in which they write *about* what they are learning, in their own voices. These notes can include evaluations of the readings, arguments that occur to them, questions they need to answer in further reading, or ideas for organizing the paper. When they begin to produce a draft, then, they will have material of their own to work with.

- *Specify a System of Documentation*

   You do not need to teach your students the detailed mechanics of documenting sources. All college handbooks of English contain complete formats at least for the MLA (Modern Language Association) system and usually for the APA (American Psychological Association) system along with sample entries and research papers. Some handbooks also include the Chicago system (which uses endnotes rather than parenthetical references in the text).

Reference librarians can guide students to source material on these formats, and the formats are also available online at many library Web sites. If you want your students to use another format specific to your discipline, you can refer them to the published guidelines for that system or tell them to look at professional journals for examples.

If you do not specify any format, however, your students will use a great variety of systems, including peculiar or inconsistent ones they improvise. If you do not care which format they use, you should at least tell them to locate and follow guidelines for a standard system. Anxiety about the details of documentation tends to distract student writers from more important attention to the quality of their writing. You can relieve some of that anxiety by reminding your students that correct documentation is really just a matter of choosing a system and following directions.

• *Comment Most Extensively on Proposals and Drafts*

Guidance you provide will have more value at the beginning of the process than at the end, even if the comments are the same. If you tell students they should refocus the topic or consult other sources in response to proposals or early portions of drafts, this advice will seem helpful, if not welcome, and could transform the paper. The same comments on a completed paper will sound like diagnoses in an autopsy.

In response to drafts, the advice we offered in Chapter 4, on revision, applies to drafts of research papers as well. Your main goal is to raise questions, make suggestions, and observe patterns that will lead the writer to assume responsibility for improving the paper. It is not your job to assume that responsibility yourself, through extensive editing and prescription. For example, if the draft of the paper needs substantial reorganization (as drafts of research papers often do), you should make this priority as clear as possible and not litter the text with minor corrections that suggest the option of cosmetic change.

• *Provide Models for the Type of Writing You Expect*

We noted that the student research paper is not in itself a specific genre of writing; nor does it correspond with any single type of published writing. A collection of research papers written for a variety of courses in different fields of study would include many kinds of reports, arguments, and analyses in differing styles and formats. If you do not specify the type of writing you want, the forms, purposes, and styles of papers in your own course will differ as well, because your students will have to invent them for the occasion or use the last papers they wrote as models.

Models for Research Papers

Providing specific examples of the kind of writing you want can greatly reduce the confusion and erratic variation in student responses to the research assignment. In highly specialized courses teachers sometimes assign investigative writing that corresponds directly with forms used in scholarship and related professions.

Sample Assignments

In his design and environmental analysis class, Cornell professor Gary Evans asks students to complete a "post-occupancy evaluation" (POE), a professional report used to determine whether the actual use of a constructed space meets the goals of its design.

In her advanced natural resources course at Cornell called Landscape Impact Analysis, Barbara Bedford assigns a complex analytical case study comparable to an environmental impact statement.

In more general, introductory courses, direct models for student research papers might be difficult to identify, but here are some of the models teachers have used in courses at various levels:

- *Research-based journalism* often serves as a good model for the style and audience of a student research paper; you can find good examples especially in periodicals intended for the educated public, such as *Psychology Today* or *Scientific American*. More general publications such as the *New Yorker* and the *Chronicle of Higher Education* also include investigative articles that might correspond with the subject of your course. Although these articles typically do not use academic documentation systems, they can show your students how to introduce references in the text of their papers, as alternatives to mysterious ("dropped") quotations and paraphrases that sound like ghostly voices in many student papers. Student research papers should maintain the clarity of reference found in investigative journalism, with citations added to identify sources more specifically.

- *Book chapters* from works of scholarship or volumes that scholars wrote for the general public can also illustrate clarity of reference along with citation. Individual chapters often discuss a specific topic within the broader subject area, with focus and length that correspond with those of student research papers.

- *Academic research articles* can work as models for student writing in some courses and fields of study, especially at high levels of instruction. Especially useful are text-based studies in fields such as history, political science, and literary studies. Experimental research articles, field studies, and complex quantitative analyses generally do not correspond with student research. And in most disciplines only certain kinds of articles in the professional literature serve as models for student papers. In an issue of *Current Anthropology*, for example, a topical, theoretical discussion of a research issue or a cross-cultural pattern could represent a type of writing feasible for undergraduates, while an ethnographic field study would not. In other words, you should refer students to specific articles or types of articles, not to whole journals.

- *Review articles* in academic journals often discuss three or four recent books or articles written about a specific topic in the field. These review articles can provide excellent examples of synthesis in the identification of central issues and questions in a highly focused area of research.

- *Research proposals* are in some ways alternatives to conventional research papers, because they describe hypothetical research that in most cases the writer cannot actually conduct. But research proposals can be a model for undergraduates, who might be able to imagine professional research without being scholars in the field. Proposals do require discussion of relevant research literature as a basis for the study proposed, and they also require the identification of a specific research question, which student research papers often fail to locate. In addition, they require some description of research methods, which advanced undergraduates can imagine using even if they can't implement the procedures. While research proposals can be valuable assignments in all fields, they are especially useful if undergraduates cannot do real research in the discipline. Because research proposals are not published, you might need to show students an example of a proposal you or one of your colleagues wrote. The introductions and methods sections of research articles also resemble proposals.

- *Imported and hybrid forms* sometimes work better than discipline-specific ones. In some cases teachers do not want student research papers to resemble professional writing in their disciplines or cannot find appropriate models in that literature. In the sciences and mathematics, for example, teachers sometimes want their students to write a kind of investigative paper that bears no resemblance to professional journal articles. In a physics or mathematics class, a historical discussion of a central problem or a biographical account of a major figure might offer an approach that best meets the teacher's goals for a research paper. A biology teacher might want students to write about issues such as the teaching of evolution in high schools or a controversy surrounding protection of an endangered species — topics that carry research into the realms of education, sociology, religion, politics, and law. You will not necessarily find close models for these types of research papers and should take special care, in that event, to describe the kind of paper you have in mind.

Creating Opportunities for Presentation and Exchange

Works of scholarship have audiences of peers, and sometimes broader audiences. As renditions of scholarship, investigative projects will be more meaningful if student writers also have an audience of peers in addition to their teacher. If they know that they will share their work with other members of the class, your students will tend to take their projects more seriously. Undergraduates want to know what other members of the class are doing, and through paper exchanges or presentations they can learn a great deal from one another. It seems a terrible waste of effort when ambitious research papers have only one reader: the professor, who probably has the least to gain from reading them.

Because the completed papers are usually due near the end of the semester, it can be difficult to arrange for students to read the finished products. In small classes teachers sometimes distribute copies of all the papers, but this is often impossible because of the volume and expense. Limited exchanges are more feasible and useful to the writers in the draft stage, through peer reviews, which we described in Chapter 4. And students can find out about all of the projects in the class through brief presentations, supplemented by visual displays or handouts. These presentations can occur before the finished papers have been turned in, during the last weeks of class, but they can also be very useful at earlier stages, when the audience can ask questions that might help bring the work into focus. Teachers sometimes schedule brief presentations of research proposals, with time for questions and discussion.

Group presentations can reduce the class time required if two or three students are working on related topics. Preparations for the presentation will also give them a chance to learn about one another's projects in some depth. Occasionally teachers give these presentations the format of a professional conference, with topical panels of student speakers. And in some science classes students present their research in a poster session, where all members of the class display visual renditions of their work. (See Chapter 8 for further discussion of student presentations.)

Advice for Preventing Plagiarism

According to several surveys, cheating of all kinds, including plagiarism, has risen steadily among high school and college students in recent years. According to different figures, 50 to 80 percent of college students admit to cheating once or more, and 30 to 50 percent say they have plagiarized from published sources or the work of other students. A related problem is that many college teachers (about half by some accounts) have stopped trying to detect and prosecute cheating. In part, plagiarism has increased through the accessibility of Internet sources and services. A teacher recently showed us a research paper draft that was a poorly assembled patchwork of material from nearly a dozen Web sites, without quotation or citation. And the students in this class had been clearly warned that the teacher would check for such practices with a Web browser.

Unfortunately, we do not have answers for the ethical questions these surveys raise, yet our view of the problem is not at all fatalistic. No one should assume, first of all, that survey percentages apply evenly and inevitably to all college courses. We suspect that there are courses in which nearly all students practice some form of plagiarism, especially on research papers. We are equally confident, however, that in some classes that include extensive writing there are no cases of plagiarism of any kind.

These extreme variations do not correspond with levels of integrity among the students. They result instead from teaching practices. Some courses, teachers, and assignments inadvertently make plagiarism inviting, even difficult to avoid; others make plagiarism virtually impossible.

To move in the latter direction you need to understand what plagiarism is, in its diverse forms, why it occurs among undergraduates, and what kinds of teaching practices make these violations of academic writing standards uninviting and unnecessary. One of the most useful responses to these questions is "Defining and Avoiding Plagiarism: The WPA Statement on Best Practices," from the Council of Writing Program Administrators (http://www.wpacouncil.org). Here we offer a briefer set of definitions and suggestions.

Types and Causes of Plagiarism

The offenses most colleges include in the loose category of "plagiarism" vary from deliberate theft and fraud to minor cases of close paraphrase and faulty reference. While all of these cases involve misrepresentation, their motivations and implications can be entirely different.

At one extreme students turn in as their own work whole papers they did not write — work copied from sources, written by other students, or downloaded from the Internet. This extreme represents conscious deception to gain unfair advantage over other students.

At the other extreme they may use "apt phrases" from references without quotation, present reworded ideas as their own, or fail to cite a reference because of faulty note taking. This extreme often results from confusion and brings neither significant advantage to the writer nor disadvantage to others.

And of course there are broad gray areas between the two extremes.

All of these forms of plagiarism are most common in research papers, though the reasons for their frequency vary. In complex projects, procrastination can easily lead to desperation. If topic selection is fairly open, Internet services, files of old papers, and student networks make it entirely too easy to find a paper that will satisfy the assignment with little alteration. And considering the time required to produce an original research paper, the deception is especially tempting.

> For reasons we have explained, however, the difficulties novice writers face in establishing an authoritative voice and position can make the task of quoting and citing real authorities very confusing. Many students therefore drift into minor forms of plagiarism because the approach they have used does not give them a sense of position from which they can easily distinguish their ideas and voices from those of other writers.

When students are writing papers directly from research notes, about perspectives they have acquired entirely from references, the answer to the question *Whose idea and language is this?* might not be at all clear.

In some cultures, furthermore, repeating what authorities say is almost a definition of learning. It is difficult for students educated in these systems to understand what it means to take an independent or original perspective, especially when they truly have learned from others everything they know about the subject, including the language required to discuss it. That dilemma is not just a cultural anomaly; it is in some ways the dilemma of all novice writers, especially when they must pretend to be experts.

How to Prevent Plagiarism

Because it is impossible to prevent all forms and cases of plagiarism, teachers often devote their attention to detection and punishment, partly in the interests of deterrence. To a great extent, however, prevention is possible, and coincides with the goals of education. *Most of the strategies we have recommended for orchestrating the research paper are also strategies for preventing plagiarism of all kinds.*

Assigning research papers in stages, for example, prevents or greatly reduces procrastination — one of the main causes of plagiarism. If students must produce proposals, lists of sources, drafted material, and other evidence of work in progress, they cannot entirely avoid the effort involved in producing the finished paper. Nor is it likely that students could locate "prewritten" research papers that correspond with the proposals and drafts they have turned in. (Only a student fully committed to deviance would locate the object of plagiarism first and produce the staged material from it.) If you meet with students to discuss their projects, they must have projects of their own to discuss.

The guidance you provide in the early stages can also prevent the more minor, less reprehensible forms of plagiarism that result from helplessness and confusion. If you help students find focused research questions, locate good sources, and revise their first approaches, they will write with a stronger sense that the paper is their own work, and not just a bunch of information they got from references. Distributing the work throughout the weeks available gives writers more time to think about the project, and those doing the thinking are the real authors. Those who haven't thought about what they are doing cannot assume real control over the material. Models for the type of writing you expect can demonstrate ways of establishing voice and handling references, and these examples are often more effective than the mechanical advice on documentation offered in textbooks.

Beyond these preventive effects of supervising research projects in stages, we have only two further suggestions for preventing plagiarism:

- *Make sure your students are aware of the risks involved in deceptive plagiarism.* Most colleges and universities distribute materials on plagiarism and other violations of integrity codes to all students, but many students do not read this material. Even if they do, they may not realize why the theft of language and ideas is such a serious offense in higher education, where "intellectual property" is the main form of currency. And they may not realize how frequently teachers recognize plagiarized material or how easily they can identify certain kinds. We suggest that you point out, for example, that Web browsers can often locate a downloaded source of a paper from a search for one sentence.

- *Link the topics for research papers closely to the content of your course.* Students will find it easier to locate "prewritten" papers, to use whole or in part, if the choice of topics is very open. Some teachers provide lists of focused topics or subject areas to limit options to familiar territory. If you do not want to impose these narrow restrictions, you can also require that papers address specific issues raised in required readings for the course, with direct reference to those readings.

All of these preventive measures will relieve the suspicions that plague teachers who simply assign research papers and collect them weeks later, with no idea how they were produced. The best prevention is real guidance and attention, which help foster the sense of trust on which good teaching and learning ultimately depend.

Links between Writing, Reading, Discussion, and Oral Presentation

Key Elements

Maximizing Personal Engagement and Collegial Interaction   122

We can think of a piece of writing not just as an individual performance but as part of an ongoing discussion that occurs through a variety of spoken and written exchanges. These lively exchanges produce some of the richest learning experiences, most valuable in the careers students will enter.

Strategies for Encouraging Effective Reading   123

The impression that college students do not know how to read usually results from the fact that they do not know why they are reading assigned texts. This lack of purpose, in turn, results from the way reading is typically assigned in undergraduate courses: as an undifferentiated, solitary activity to be completed for the vague purpose of knowing what the text contains.

If you expect your students to read assigned material in particular ways, you should make those expectations clear:

- Include purposes in all reading assignments.
- Explain the central purpose of the reading assignment.
- Describe future uses of the text.
- Annotate reading assignments.
- Link reading assignments with discussion and writing.
- Limit the amount of reading you assign.

Maximizing Personal Engagement and Collegial Interaction

In Chapter 1, on course design, we encouraged you to think of writing not as an isolated activity or skill but as one medium of communication interwoven with others — reading, speaking, and listening — in the whole fabric of your course. We argued that these related uses of language primarily determine the kinds and qualities of learning that occur. If students are just listening to lectures, reading assigned texts, and taking notes to prepare for exams, they will learn the material in ways appropriate for that purpose of demonstrating knowledge on exams. Formal writing assignments can also function essentially as examinations: tests of the individual student's grasp of knowledge acquired through lectures and assigned readings.

But writing can function in many other relations to learning, in ways linked with reading, speaking, and listening. In the sciences, engineering, and other fields, writing is one component of the broader category of *communication*, which includes skills in speaking and listening, often in collaboration with others. Another term that expresses these relations is *discourse*, which refers broadly to the exchange of ideas and information through discussion, both in writing and in speech.

> We can therefore think of a piece of writing not just as an individual performance but as part of an ongoing discussion that occurs through a variety of spoken and written exchanges: dialogues, class discussions, debates, formal presentations, and informal writing. These lively exchanges produce some of the richest learning experiences, most valuable in the careers students will enter. Knowing how to participate constructively in these discussions is an essential kind of learning in itself, and one that is often neglected in higher education.

In *Making the Most of College*, Richard Light suggests that the extraordinary learning experiences undergraduates attribute to foreign language classes do not result entirely from the benefits of learning foreign languages, great as these benefits are. He believes instead that students rate language classes so highly because they include features that would enrich any course: active, interactive forms of writing, reading, speaking, and listening in lively association with teachers and other students. "I believe the big message from these findings," Light concludes, "is that students are enthusiastic when classes are structured to maximize personal engagement and collegial interaction" (80).

This conclusion has been the basis for many of our suggestions in previous chapters on course design (Chapter 1), writing assignments (Chapter 2), and informal writing (Chapter 5). Here we will focus more closely on strategies for using active reading, lively discussion, and oral presentations to enrich writing and for using writing to enrich reading, discussion, and presentations — and consequently to enrich learning.

Strategies for Encouraging Effective Reading

Our Professional Purposes and Strategies for Reading

Writing and reading are closely related in higher education, in part because so much academic writing is based on publications in a field of study. Academic books and articles invariably contain references to other books and articles on the subject. The significance of what we have to say as writers emerges in relation to other work we have read, in complex frames of reference. Writing and reading are also linked with presentations and discussions at academic conferences and with informal exchanges of many kinds through which scholars define their positions in relation to other scholars in their disciplines.

"My field," one biochemist told us, "is a beehive of communication."

Within these beehives of communication we write as readers, and we often read as writers, for the purpose of completing articles or books that contribute to a field of inquiry, knowledge, and discussion. Like academic writing, academic reading is therefore a rhetorical activity — or more accurately a variety of activities, differentiated by specific reasons for reading something at a particular time. When undergraduates see hundreds of books and periodicals in our offices, they assume that we have read most of this material from cover to cover and intend to read the rest in the same fashion. In fact, we have read some of this literature closely, perhaps several times, focusing on specific chapters, articles, or passages. Yet many of the books and journals on our shelves we haven't opened at all or have only glanced at in passing. We keep much of this work on hand for reference, so we can find specific information to use in writing or teaching. When "reading" issues of journals, we might scan the table of contents or leaf through the issue to identify interesting articles, while ignoring others. Even when we find articles of importance we do not necessarily read them from beginning to end. We might look at the introduction and conclusion, read the abstract, or focus on tables and other figures. We examine some books or articles with intense critical scrutiny, and we read others with more open, receptive interest. All of these strategies and others serve specific purposes for reading, linked with writing, research, and teaching.

In a particular instance, therefore, knowing how to read something results almost automatically from knowing why we are reading, and without some purpose reading is an aimless activity. A gripping novel might sustain continuous reading simply for entertainment or diversion, but these are still motivations that determine the way we read a novel: typically from the first word to the last, without deliberate effort to learn or remember what the book contains.

Undergraduates' Limited Purposes and Strategies for Reading

We begin with these general observations because college teachers so often complain that their students do not know how to read assigned texts. And if these teachers believe that undergraduates should have learned to write effectively in high school, they are more likely to believe that their students should know how to read assigned material without instruction. Reading, even more than writing, seems a "basic skill" all students should have acquired before they entered college. College teachers therefore view the necessity of "teaching reading" as a remedial form of instruction beneath the level of college work. Yet the apparent need for this kind of teaching persists.

We offer an alternative view of the problem of "teaching reading," one that does not require the deliberate teaching of reading skills: the impression that college students do not know *how* to read usually results from the fact that they do not know *why* they are reading assigned texts. This lack of purpose, in turn, results from the way reading is typically assigned in undergraduate courses: as an undifferentiated, solitary activity to be completed for the vague purpose of knowing what the text contains.

Here is an example of a reading assignment from a typical course syllabus:

Week 6: Read Hinton, Ch. VI, pp. 142–86; Carlson, Ch. III, pp. 63–104.

Why should students read these chapters, or other assigned texts? There are many possible answers to this question:

- to understand lectures
- to memorize information that might appear on exams
- to get a general sense of the content of the text
- to analyze the structure of the text, the way it was written
- to identify the author's position on an issue
- to develop one's own position on the subject
- to correlate the content with other readings and issues in the course
- to participate in a class discussion on the topic
- to locate specific information for a broader research project
- to write a critical analysis of the text
- to write a paper on a related topic

DIFFERENTIATED READING STRATEGIES These specific reasons for reading the assignment favor different methods, to varying degrees linear or nonlinear, critical or accepting, analytical or holistic, thorough or cursory. For some purposes it might make sense for students to spend only a few minutes identifying the author's central argument in an essay. For other purposes they might need to spend an hour or two reading the same essay very thoroughly, more than once, while making notes for future reference in papers or discussions; these notes might emphasize what the author has said, or they might help the reader construct counterarguments. All of these strategies require the development of reading skills, but they develop only through practice, when we give students explicit reasons for reading in specific ways.

UNDIFFERENTIATED, LINEAR READING STRATEGIES If we give students undifferentiated reading assignments, they in turn will develop undifferentiated methods of reading that become habitual when most of their reading assignments are vague requirements. Told simply to read a textbook chapter for a certain week, most students will revert to a passive, linear method used simply to familiarize themselves with the material and prepare for further study, should some specific purpose arise. Highlighter in hand, they will start to read at the beginning of the chapter and proceed to the end, marking portions that seem important. While this method serves some purposes — such as understanding lectures or preparing for exams — it does not develop critical and analytical perspectives, prepare students for active participation in discussions, or lay the groundwork for writing about the material.

EFFECTS OF READING STRATEGIES ON CLASS DISCUSSION To the extent that students use other reading methods, their grasp of the material will vary in unpredictable ways that can undermine cohesion in the class. In a class discussion of an essay, for example, some students will be prepared only to tell you in general terms what the author said. Others will be able to analyze the components of the writer's argument, without developing positions of their own, while some students might react critically to specific points without developing a general understanding of the author's position. Discussion will therefore become fragmented and difficult to lead.

Ways to Encourage Effective Reading

As the preceding discussion has indicated, if you expect your students to read assigned material in particular ways, you should make those expectations clear. This means that you must first identify those expectations when you design your course and assignments. Our central argument is that it is not sufficient for teachers to decide *what* they want students to read. If you assign specific texts you should also know, and let your students know, what purposes these texts will serve in relation to the structure and goals of your course.

To be integral features of learning and discourse, reading assignments should be explicitly linked with discussion, writing, and other components of a course.

INCLUDE PURPOSES IN ALL READING ASSIGNMENTS If you establish a rule that you must always explain to students why you are asking them to read something, you will recognize that assigned texts serve a variety of purposes. And even if those functions seem obvious to you, they will not be obvious to your students, who are typically unfamiliar with the literature in your field. Several kinds of information can help students develop appropriate reading strategies.

EXPLAIN THE CENTRAL PURPOSE OF THE READING ASSIGNMENT   Even if assigned chapters or articles serve the general purpose of developing basic knowledge of the subject, you should explain that goal along with the reasons for which students might need this information, in and beyond your class. For example, a reading assignment might include the comment "You will need to read this chapter thoroughly to understand specific cases we discuss next week."

DESCRIBE FUTURE USES OF THE TEXT   Some readings will have multiple functions that require different ways of reading at different times in the course, and students will appreciate any advice you can offer about the uses you have in mind for this material in the future. Your assignment might encourage students to read a text more than once, and in different ways, as the term progresses.

Sample Assignment

Read Chapter VI in Hinton as a basis first for understanding the cases we discuss next week. We will return to this chapter when you write a comparison between Hinton's theory and Caldwell's two weeks later, and an understanding of both theories will serve you well in the midterm exam.

ANNOTATE READING ASSIGNMENTS   We tend to assume that the nature and significance of texts we assign will be self-evident to students when they read these texts, but they may not be self-evident to readers unfamiliar with a field of study. Many of us have assigned an essay because the author's position was questionable and found that our students read it as gospel truth. When we choose specific readings, we have extensive background knowledge about their authors, intellectual traditions, and surrounding debates; our student readers will benefit from our sharing some of this information. In other words, they will know *how* to read more effectively if they know not only *why* they are reading but also *what* they are reading.

These explanations resemble bibliographic annotations, which might explain the author's status in the field, along with the function and reputation of the work: whether it is a general survey, a widely accepted basis for subsequent research, a representation of a particular school of thought, a controversial new approach, or an old theory that has been widely challenged. This information will also encourage awareness of the connections and contrasts among the texts you assign.

Sample Assignment

In a syllabus entry for his course Religion, Ethics, and the Environment, Professor Richard Baer in the field of natural resources included annotation, along with advice about reading level and strategy:

> Ian G. Barbour, *Issues in Science and Religion*, pp. 137–85. For those of you who have had little or no background in philosophy, this will be difficult material. The assignment is short, but you may need to read it two or three times to really understand it. The material is a bit dated, but it remains, in my judgment, one of the best short discussions of what it means to know something in science.

LINK READING ASSIGNMENTS WITH DISCUSSION AND WRITING   You can also encourage active, analytical reading by including in your assignments specific questions your students should attempt to answer. The questions can serve as a basis for class discussions and writing assignments, but they also enrich the activity of reading itself, by offering analytical tools for distinguishing components of the work or by suggesting connections among readings and issues in the course.

We can't reasonably expect students to read actively if reading has no active function in writing, dialogue, or discussion. In writing or writing-intensive classes, or in any class taught as a seminar, reading, writing, and discussion should be vitally connected components of discourse, in lively associations that constitute learning in the course. In such classes there is little reason for students to read assigned texts only to absorb the contents in a silent repository of personal knowledge. They should read always with a sense of outcome — with intentions linked with writing and discussion.

In a writing class, these active uses of language often merge to the extent that reading assignments, writing assignments, and discussion topics are indistinguishable. Students are always reading specific texts for the purposes of formal and informal writing or for participation in class discussions. Yet there are some benefits in making these different functions clear in the assignments themselves.

Sample Assignment

In her writing seminar on the politics of corruption, political scientist Elizabeth Remick listed in her syllabus not only the readings assigned for each week but also discussion questions used as a guide for reading, writing assignments linked with these readings, and related in-class activities. She elaborated and revised these guidelines as the term progressed.

For week 4, for example, Remick assigned sections (each about thirty pages) from two books on the week's topic of tax farming in prerevolutionary China and France. (Tax farming was the common practice of subcontracting revenue collection for regions to the highest bidders, who could then keep the excess they squeezed from the populations.) Beneath the reading assignment she listed questions to guide reading in preparation for class discussions and writing:

> Discussion Topic: Is this corruption? Was this corruption at the time? Is there anything intrinsically wrong with tax farming? Or does any state that doesn't have a big bureaucracy or a lot of money have to use this method of revenue collection? What would happen if someone tried tax farming now in the U.S.?

In addition to class discussion of these questions, Remick scheduled a "writing workshop" on revising, with peer review of the first drafts of the previous week's assignment, on the nature of corruption in a different historical context.

To the extent that questions like Remick's narrow reading, they do so in ways that stimulate and focus active reading, along with awareness of connections between texts. If they are trying to answer questions that extend beyond the individual readings, students are more likely to think of these texts as related cases in the understanding of larger issues. In fact, the question *Is this corruption?* was a central theme throughout the term, used to build a broad, critical understanding of corruption in political systems. If they read for the purpose of answering these questions — not just to absorb content — students will also enter class discussions with positions they can exchange, and these exchanges will enrich the writing they later produce.

Without making these direct links between reading, writing, and discussion, teachers have very little sense of the ways in which students are completing reading assignments or whether they are reading the material at all.

Sample Assignments

To address the problem of knowing how students were completing and using reading assignments in a course on the sociology of marriage, sociologists Marin Clarkberg and Kristen Schultz asked their students, at the beginning of each class, to respond in writing to questions about the reading assignments. These responses formed the basis for class discussions and were collected at the end of the period. This in-class writing was also averaged into the students' grades for participation, because Clarkberg and Schultz viewed this writing, like spoken discussion, as contributions to the exchange of ideas. This practice encouraged students to think of reading, writing, and discussion as interwoven threads of discourse and participation in the dynamics of the class.

In their writing-intensive sections of an evolution course for biology majors, Susi Remold and Colleen Webb used periodic "Writing on Fundamentals" assignments to link general concepts covered in the assigned readings and lectures with the analysis of specific cases. Each of these assignments offered students a choice between two cases, or "scenarios," to which they should apply a general concept in evolutionary biology. In "Writing on Fundamentals #1," for example, the first scenario described the peculiar phenomenon of gastric breeding in two species of frogs, whose young develop in the mother's stomach. The second scenario concerned the ability of anemone fish to defeat the potentially deadly response to intruders in the tentacles of sea anemones, which then provide refuge to these little fish from predators. For both scenarios the question for writing elicited an informal research proposal:

> *Question: In two double-spaced pages or less, describe how you would determine whether or not evolution by natural selection is occurring in your chosen scenario. Be sure to give your definitions of natural selection and evolution. Describe what questions you would need to answer about your organisms in order to determine whether evolution by natural selection is occurring. In addition, you can think about what experiment(s) you could do to answer those questions.*

Many other types of informal writing we described in Chapter 5 also link reading with discussion and writing in the fabric of a course. If you assign course journals, for example, you can require entries on reading assignments. Like study questions and reading notes, these journal entries can help prepare students for class discussions and form the basis for formal papers. E-mail lists can focus on issues related to reading assignments, in ways that encourage active, strategic reading. As we suggested, you can also ask students to formulate tentative, written positions on issues before they read assigned texts. These position statements encourage students to approach readings with a sense of direction and to read from a critical perspective.

LIMIT THE AMOUNT OF READING YOU ASSIGN   Guidelines for first-year writing seminars in the disciplines at Cornell limit assigned reading to no more than seventy-five pages per week, preferably less. This restriction resulted from the common tendency of teachers to equate extensive reading with "coverage" and mastery of the subject. After all, we are authorities in these fields partly because we have read so much, and by comparison undergraduates in our courses have read almost nothing. In planning our courses, when we think of what students need to learn in order to write intelligently about the topic, we immediately think of all the books and articles they should read. How can they write about *Hamlet* without reading several of the other tragedies? How can they write with any real understanding of Shakespeare's plays without also reading some of the comedies, the sonnets, and critical studies of his work? With the best intentions, we want to compress years of scholarship into a few weeks of instruction.

But this is a lost cause. Given the limiting factor of time, the relationship between reading and learning is governed by the Raspberry Jam Principle: the wider you spread it, the thinner it gets. If you assign too much reading, your students will not have time to develop a deep understanding through writing and discussion or to make connections among widely dispersed perspectives.

Teachers who assign the most reading are most likely to complain that they can't find time to discuss course topics and student writing in class or work with the development and revision of essays. They also complain that their students do not read assigned texts thoroughly.

As Peter Elbow argues in his essay "The War between Reading and Writing - - and How to End It," this problem occurs throughout the undergraduate curriculum, as a result of the "root metaphor" for learning: that *"learning is input —* 'taking things in' — putting things inside us. People think of root activities in school," Elbow says, "as listening and reading, not talking and writing" (12). Considering the importance of talking and writing in the professions our students enter, this idea of learning puts higher education at odds with what our students call the "real world."

In a writing class, an imbalance toward reading built into the design of your course can undermine its goals for the rest of the term. We therefore recommend that you require students to read only the central texts they will have time to read thoroughly, discuss in class, and use as references in their writing.

Beyond these required readings, it can be useful to give students access to a wider range of literature that enriches understanding of the subject. You can do this by differentiating the readings you include in your syllabus and assignments. Clearly distinguish the central, required texts you assign from the supplementary, recommended readings students can consult as further references in their papers or to pursue further interest in the topic.

Strategies for Encouraging Good Discussion

We have already suggested strategies for linking writing and reading assignments with class discussion. Study questions and other informal writing, completed in or outside class, will help prepare students for productive, focused discussion of readings and central issues in your course. These preparations will also draw a wider range of students into participation and will reduce the influence of individuals who tend to dominate discussions.

Nevertheless, it would be misleading to suggest that teachers can entirely control classroom dynamics or that we should even try to do so. After all, the easiest way to control what happens in class is to reduce our students to silence and thus eliminate dynamics altogether. To the extent that we encourage students to speak and interact, we also relinquish some measure of control over what happens: who will speak, what they will say, and what direction the discussion will take.

Inexperienced instructors, and experienced instructors accustomed to teaching lecture courses, often approach class discussion with a kind of hopeful trepidation. *When I stop speaking or ask a question*, they wonder, *what will happen next?* The response or silence that follows seems to be governed by a mysterious chemistry that changes unpredictably from one semester to another — even from one day to the next. Some classes are filled with lively, talkative students who enjoy discussion. Others resemble what one high school teacher called "Village of the Damned," from the vintage horror movie in which children without souls stare blankly through hollow, expressionless eyes. More often our classes contain both types of students, in varying proportions, and we struggle to silence some of them while encouraging others to participate. Yet these efforts to moderate discussion have their own effects. To the extent that we intervene to focus or distribute responses, we also draw attention to ourselves, and this is not necessarily where we want attention to fall.

Considering all of the unpredictable factors in play, the quality of discussion in a particular class period can seem to be the result of chance more than of design. Elaborate plans can sometimes reduce the quantity and quality of student participation. Open discussions, in turn, sometimes work beautifully and on other occasions produce aimless, fragmented exchange. As a consequence, teachers often question the value of interactive learning or simply hope for the best.

While we can't offer foolproof methods for regulating effective discussions, we can clarify some of the general principles of classroom dynamics involved and offer a few suggestions for encouraging constructive participation in class.

OBSERVE PRINCIPLES OF "WAIT TIME"   One factor you can control is the extent to which *you* speak — and how and when. In her review article on studies of "wait time," Mary Budd Rowe notes that "when teachers ask questions of students, they typically wait 1 second or less for the students to start a reply; after the student stops speaking they begin their reaction or proffer the next question in less than 1 second" (43).

Why should we wait longer (given the agony of silence) or slow the pace of instruction generally? Analysis of student responses reveals that when teachers increase "wait time" from one second to three seconds or more — both after they ask questions and after students respond — significant changes occur in the quality of responses and in the quality of the class in general. Rowe reports ten varieties of change:

1. "The length of student responses increases between 300% and 700%."

2. "More inferences are supported by evidence and logical argument."

3. "The incidence of speculative thinking increases."

4. Students ask more questions and offer more spontaneous suggestions.

5. Interaction in the class increases.

6. "Failures to respond decrease."

7. Students become more attentive and less restless.

8. More students participate voluntarily.

9. Students speak with greater confidence and with fewer inflections on the order of "Is that what you want?" or "Well, I'm not sure, but. . . ."

10. "Achievement improves on written measures [e.g., essay exams] where the items are cognitively complex." (45)

When teachers become accustomed to pauses, both before and after student responses, their roles in the classroom also change. Rowe reports that they respond to students with greater flexibility and less "mimicry" (the repetition and rephrasing of a student's response); they become engaged in more complex and sustained discussions with students; and they take a wider range of students into account: "some previously 'invisible' people become visible" (45).

The main value of this research lies in the evidence that, in their effort to make discussions work, by filling silence, teachers often prevent discussion from working because they continually interrupt thought and response. In practice, however, wait time is not a formula for good discussion, but a variable that alters with teaching styles, course designs, and classroom activities. You might not ask the questions, or you might remain silent for most of the period during discussions, debates, or presentations. It's useful to pause most deliberately and longest at the beginning of a semester and at the beginning of a class period: the very times when teachers are most inclined and students are least inclined to talk. When you feel that you need to get things rolling and take charge, you usually need instead to slow down and get out of the way. If students think of the teacher as narrator and of themselves as a homogeneous, passive audience, even three seconds of silence will produce little more than mounting tension. This tension will linger as a sense of failure if you break it by answering your own question and thus reaffirm your role as the one person in the class who has all the answers. While we do need to leave room for student participation, a wide range of factors influences the quality of that participation.

DISCUSS THE GOALS AND RULES FOR DISCUSSION   One of these factors is students' conception of discussion itself. On the basis of a study
she conducted at Grinnell College, Carol Trosset suggests that unsuccessful discussions, especially on sensitive issues, often result from implicit conflicts between the teacher's goals and assumptions and those
of students. Through interviews with more than two hundred undergraduates, Trosset found that the majority of students held particular
views of discussion that could undermine the kinds of exchange most
instructors value: the exploratory consideration of ideas put out on the
table, in a spirit of inquiry.

In contrast to teachers' views, here are the main student views
Trosset found:

- The majority viewed participation in discussion as advocacy of a
  strongly held position. If they did not have a strong position or
  did not want to advocate one, they felt they should remain silent.

- Students believed the goal of discussion was consensus, and for
  this reason they often viewed disagreement and difference as
  negative factors. For example, 75 percent said they preferred to
  discuss diversity issues "with people of the same views or background as themselves" (47).

- Most believed that personal experience was the main or only
  "source of legitimate knowledge." For example, many said that
  women are in a position to discuss sexism, while men are not.
  "This bias," Trosset observes, "both forces members of less powerful groups into the role of peer instructors, and supports the
  impression that members of more powerful groups have nothing
  to say" (47).

- Many students believed that they had a right to express views
  without being challenged.

- From the position of "radical relativism," they often argued that
  every view is just an "opinion," to which everyone has a right.
  Their conception of tolerance was therefore based on the premise
  that all views are equally valid.

- The great majority said that feeling comfortable was an important basis for discussion. Fear of causing discomfort was therefore a reason for remaining silent.

Such ideas can severely limit exploratory discussions in which participants test and exchange tentative ideas, with concern for reasoning
and evidence. "Critical thinking," which all colleges proclaim to be a
central goal of instruction, is virtually impossible if personal experience is the basis for validity and if all opinions are equally valid.

We cannot effectively legislate our own views of what a good discussion should become, but we can make this question a topic of dis-

cussion early in the term and explain our own goals. In fact, Trosset's article can be a useful reading assignment to get these issues on the table for negotiation.

GIVE STUDENTS TIME TO BE WHERE THEY ARE   We suggested that giving students a few minutes at the beginning of class to respond in writing to discussion topics improves the range and quality of participation. This exercise, among others, also gives students time to realize they are in your class and not somewhere else. When they take their seats around a seminar table, many students have just spent the past hour silently listening (and perhaps dozing) in the back of a lecture hall, where they were essentially invisible. You might notice that when they arrive in your class they look like they are still in the back of a lecture hall, disposed only to watch and listen, not to speak.

The beginning of a class period is therefore a crucial time that strongly influences the interaction that follows. As an alternative to writing at this time, you can begin with casual conversation to establish the tone for discussion, or ask a question that everyone can answer and go around the room quickly so all students have a chance to speak. For similar purposes, some teachers begin by dividing the class into smaller groups to discuss a question and then reconvene for reports on what they said. This practice gets everyone talking from the beginning of the period, and having conversed in small groups they are more likely to contribute to a general discussion.

TAKE RESPONSIBILITY FOR INCLUSIVE, CONSTRUCTIVE SEATING ARRANGEMENTS   Teachers often have a fatalistic attitude toward classroom configurations and seating patterns. If they have been assigned a classroom with fixed seating in rows for a course that emphasizes discussion, they just try to make do with the arrangement. When their students settle into seating patterns that discourage participation, they feel reluctant to move people around.

But seating arrangements can have profound effects on the quality of your class, and in the worst cases can make good discussions impossible.

What can you do about seating arrangements?

- If you've been assigned a classroom inappropriate for discussion, it will be worth your trouble to request a better room.

- If some of your students always sit together with a vow of silence or obstruction, make them sit in different places.

- If shy or disaffected students sit off in the margins of the group, with the hope of remaining in the background, insist that they move up to the table or into the circle.

- Working in small groups or in pairs forces a rearrangement of seating if you form the groups and tell them to convene in particular places.

- You can also encourage students to move around simply by sitting in different places each day, rather than habitually taking the same position. If you have a predictable position, students will assume it's at the head of the class.

- Ideally, you and your students should be able to see one another, either around a table or in a circle of chairs. To encourage interaction, you should sit among your students as a fellow participant, rather than standing over them or presiding at the head of the table.

VARY THE CLASS FORMAT AND ACTIVITIES   Class discussions can become stale or disorganized as the period or semester progresses because teachers are thinking of discussion as one kind of activity: the open exchange of ideas in the entire class. In fact, good discussions come in many forms, and even in a small class, animated, self-directed conversation is difficult to sustain. How often do we have intense, intellectual, hour-long conversations with our best friends? How often do our own staff and committee meetings represent the lively, focused exchanges we expect from our students? We shouldn't be surprised if such discussions are harder to achieve with a class of fifteen or twenty students or if the topics sometimes drift just as aimlessly as our own conversations often do.

Students are more likely to remain engaged in productive exchanges if we vary the kinds of discussion and other activity during a class period and throughout the term.

In addition to general discussions, variations on activities can include

- work in pairs or small groups
- formal debates between two teams
- brief periods of informal writing or individual work on drafts
- peer review sessions
- student-led discussions
- field trips
- guest presentations with discussion periods
- opportunities for students to read their papers aloud
- other kinds of student presentations

In some of these activities you will need to take charge of the class and tell students very clearly what to do. In others you will need to get out of the way and let the students take responsibility. Sometimes, as in small-group activities, you need to do both: first provide very clear instructions for the activity and then get out of the way.

GIVE STUDENTS RESPONSIBILITY FOR LEADING DISCUSSIONS
Student-led discussions seem like a particularly risky enterprise, even for teachers who like the idea in principle. If we have trouble getting our students to participate actively in class, how can we expect them to take responsibility for this difficult kind of instruction?

If students receive guidance and time for preparation, however, they usually do a surprisingly good job of eliciting discussion from their classmates. Some excellent teachers have told us that the most lively interaction occurred when their students were leading the class.

Students rise to this occasion for several reasons. Given real responsibility for the class, they don't want to let you down. But perhaps more compellingly, they don't want to let their classmates down by leading a boring or chaotic class. As a rule, furthermore, the classmates are very supportive, cooperative, and responsive, partly because they want this support when their turn to lead the class arrives. Through a healthy spirit of competitive performance, successive sessions tend to get better.

Teachers who believe that good discussions rely on their own authority and direction of the class can be disillusioned by the lively exchanges their students elicit, while they sit quietly at the back of the room. In fact, one teacher with a strong work ethic came to us for reassurance toward the end of the term, when his students had been leading the class for a couple of weeks and he wasn't doing very much. For those who feel they are doing too much, however, getting out of the limelight can be an enormous relief.

Successful student-led discussions, however, do not happen automatically. Some basic principles will improve the odds that these sessions will work.

- *Choose teams of two or three students to lead the class.* Solo performances are more daunting, and the students can make better plans if they pool their ideas and abilities. If you want to give everyone this opportunity, furthermore, team presentations will reduce the number of periods required.

- *Schedule all presentations well in advance and meet with the teams to discuss their topics and strategies.* Teachers sometimes assign topics to the groups and provide lists of resources.

- *Schedule student-led discussions in the last half of the term, not the first.* Students will not be able to lead discussions effectively until they have learned substantial amounts about the subject and are familiar with the class.

- *Elicit possible topics from the class at large.* Some teachers ask all of their students each week to submit interesting questions from readings and previous classes. These are sent by e-mail to the teacher and to the discussion leaders for the following week. In consultation with the teacher, the leaders choose the most interesting and important questions as topics for their session.

- *Encourage the teams to develop creative strategies for engaging interest and participation.* One colleague recently told us that a pair of discussion leaders in his class staged a brief, vigorous argument, taking opposite positions on an issue, and then competed to bring classmates over to their sides — literally on different sides of the room. The session evolved into a large-scale debate between two factions.

- *Require classmates to give the discussion leaders constructive feedback after the sessions.* The leaders will want to know, and will benefit from knowing, what worked and what did not. Classmates will benefit too from articulating these strengths and weaknesses, for their own sessions or for future occasions.

- *When student-led classes start, stay in the background as much as possible.*

Because students learn from one another as the sessions progress, there are disadvantages to going first, especially if the teams are graded for the quality of their work. One teacher offered some bonus points to the team that volunteered to go first, to compensate for this disadvantage.

For obvious reasons, student-led discussions will not work in every course. The class must be fairly small to allow time for everyone to lead a session; even in a small class, time constraints might make these sessions impossible, especially if your class includes other kinds of student-centered activities, such as presentations or readings.

Strategies for Effective Oral Presentations

Student-led discussions and oral presentations overlap in form and function, and oral presentations themselves vary considerably — from brief, informal readings or reviews to formal presentations on ambitious research projects. We should also note that oral presentations take very different forms among academic disciplines, as we can observe from attending professional conferences. Scholars in the humanities typically give individual presentations (though often on topical panels) in which they read a prepared text. Owing to the collaborative nature of their research, scientists often give team presentations, with extensive visual aids, and speak about the topic from a few notes at most. These differences influence the kinds of student presentation teachers find appropriate in their courses.

Yet all forms of presentation offer some common benefits to students and to the quality of a course:

- They are all types of performance that place students and their work, if only briefly, at the center of attention.

- For the duration of that performance, students hold full responsibility for the quality of the class.

- They offer students a real outcome for their writing, reading, and research.

- Both the presenter and the audience benefit from sharing finished projects or work in progress.

- Given this opportunity to read or describe their work, students can get excellent feedback from one another.

- The necessity of preparing clear, well-organized presentations can greatly improve writing on the topic, especially if revision occurs after the presentation.

- Presentations give students valuable practice and guidance in types of communication that are important in almost every career.

Considering these potential benefits, oral presentations are usually worth the class time they require, but to realize this value you want to help students' performances go as well as possible. During the presentations, as in student-led discussions, you should remain in the background. In preparation stages, however, students need and deserve guidance, to help ensure that they and their audiences have good experiences. This guidance is especially important for high-stakes presentations that require a lot of class time and constitute a large portion of the grade. If you ask students to assume the responsibility for presentations, even for five or ten minutes of class time, you hold responsibility, to them and to other students, for helping them make the best use of that time. For you as for the presenters, this is not an occasion for shyness.

Here we briefly describe some types of presentations teachers have used productively in their courses.

- *Reading papers aloud, either in finished form or in drafts.* Tell students they should read clearly and not too quickly. Distribute copies of the paper in advance, so the audience can see the text and make notes for discussion while they listen.

- *Proposals for writing or research.* Because constructive criticism and suggestions from the audience are the main goals of the presentation, speakers should present their ideas very concisely with strict time limits of five or ten minutes. Schematic representations such as projections or handouts are especially useful for this purpose and serve as references for discussion.

- *Summaries and reviews of specific articles — or "journal club."* Following a practice common in research groups and some graduate programs, teachers ask individual students or teams to choose an article (or essay, short story, or poem) for the entire class to read, to present a brief, critical summary of the text, and then to lead a discussion of its significance.

You will need to recommend methods of finding material, review the students' choices of readings to make sure they are appropriate, and if necessary suggest alternatives. Offer to answer questions, review plans, and resolve problems. Make sure the other students know they must read the assigned texts in advance and be prepared to discuss them.

- *Panel presentations, or symposia.* Based on the models of professional conferences, these panels are composed of students who have studied and written about related topics. Their individual presentations, with discussion following, usually take an entire class period. Some teachers base these presentations on submitted papers, read and respond to drafts in the roles of journal editors or conference organizers, and compile the revised papers in "proceedings" distributed to the class.

  Students should submit proposals and drafts of their papers for your review and/or peer review. If you do not want them simply to read their papers (which should have strict word limits), you will need to provide guidelines for the kind of "talk" you expect, as with other presentations described here. To moderate the pace of the presentations, you can serve as the panel "chair": introducing the speakers, keeping them within time constraints, and calling for questions from the audience.

- *Position papers.* Individual students or teams develop positions on issues raised in the course and present arguments to the class, based on assigned readings and further research. These can be dispassionate arguments or highly persuasive ones, designed to convince the audience and defeat other positions, as in debate.

  As in panel presentations, the oral argument might differ from the written version. But if you require at least drafts of the paper in advance, you will have opportunities to make suggestions relevant to the presentation as well. You should also review plans for the oral presentation and give some general guidelines to the class, including instructions to the audience about their roles and responsibilities in discussion. Some teachers ask students to revise the written version after the presentation, to benefit from discussion and other feedback.

- *Poster sessions.* These presentations are standard features of science conferences, but teachers in other fields will probably remember them from high school science fairs. Students prepare visual material and demonstrations on their research topics and stand at tables to explain this material to those who attend the session. Poster sessions can be appropriate, efficient forms of presentation in all kinds of undergraduate courses that include research projects. They are efficient because many or all of the students in the class can present their projects at once, either individually or in teams. Posters usually include considerable amounts of writing, in combination with visual aids and speech.

Poster sessions require you to organize the event and also to supervise the development of posters and demonstrations. If possible you should also make these public events, open to members of your department or to other students. If this is impossible, hold two sessions, so that half the class can be the audience for the event. Writing assignments can be tied to these sessions. For example, teachers sometimes require students to take notes and write summary descriptions of two of the poster presentations they visited. This encourages attentiveness and questions from the audience.

- *Formal research reports.* These individual or team presentations report on completed research projects, which are presented also in written form; the formal reports require from ten to thirty minutes or more. They usually occur toward the end of the term and include visual aids such as overhead projections and handouts.

  Especially if they involve teams, these formal presentations require extensive guidance from the teacher, which we describe separately (p. 157). Many undergraduates have never given a formal presentation on research and will not be aware of basic requirements for planning and delivery. If possible, arrange for interested guests (other teachers, administrators, or students) to attend these presentations. Tell presenters they can invite friends.

When students are preparing team presentations you should meet with them to discuss their plans or at least review written accounts of their intentions. For individuals and groups, however, some general guidelines in advance can save you and your students considerable time and worry, and good guidelines will greatly improve the quality of the performances. Even the most obvious advice can be useful.

Possible Presentation Guidelines for Students

- Adhere strictly to time limitations, both for your group and for individual portions.
- Make very clear, concrete plans for individual roles in team presentations.
- Determine who will manage the visual aids, such as PowerPoint screens, overheads, or distribution of handouts.
- Practice your presentations, to improve delivery and calculate timing.
- Maintain eye contact with the audience.

- Do not stand in front of your projections or turn around to refer to them.

- Avoid reading or repeating information presented on visuals.

- Speak clearly and not too quickly.

- Work to eliminate habitual, meaningless pauses such as "Um . . . well . . . ah . . . like . . . you know. . . ."

- Think of this as a pleasurable opportunity to explain your research to an interested audience.

Feedback for and Grading of Presentations

Brief, informal presentations, such as readings, are not graded as a rule or figure only in course grades for participation. By contrast, formal presentations on research can constitute a substantial portion of the course grade, either separately or combined with the research paper on the topic. In these combined writing and presentation projects, as we have noted, the presentation should occur when the research and a draft of the paper are complete, but ideally before the draft is revised. Some teachers distribute drafts of the research paper to the audience in advance of the presentation, and the opportunity for revision provides additional justification for peer evaluations of this work.

In any case, student presenters will benefit from and usually welcome extensive feedback on their performances, from you and from their classmates. As in many forms of presentation, professional models for this feedback can serve as a guide. Audiences at professional conferences typically fill out brief evaluation sheets on individual sessions. You can produce versions of these forms for distribution at the sessions, with relevant questions about content and delivery. These evaluations can be useful in grading, and presenters should receive copies for their own benefit.

"Controlled Drift"

Speaking at once of canoeing, teaching, and living, a colleague once described the ideal of "controlled drift": the pleasure of gently, almost effortlessly steering, letting the current provide the momentum and general direction, with leisurely attention to the places it takes you. For many of us these are the most enjoyable, relaxing experiences in the classroom, when the discussion carries everyone along with its own momentum and we gently steer, when necessary, into the most promising channels or to avoid running aground. It's the flow of interaction, not our effort to create interaction, that carries the discussion from one place to another.

In such classes, students and teachers are all participants, and the divisions among writing, reading, speaking, listening, and thinking also diminish. While students listen and think, they are always on the verge of speech as we are in conversation, when confusion, doubt, and disagreement are not barriers to speech but occasions for exchange. In this kind of class, students listen as speakers and they speak as listeners, in response to others. Writing and reading also become integral parts of this exchange, both as results of discussion and as topics for discussion. These interrelated uses of language supply the energy that keeps the class in motion. And to the extent that everyone is participating in these uses of language, responsibility, effort, and satisfaction are equally distributed.

This is the kind of teaching experience most of us want, especially in a course that emphasizes writing and discussion. In any case, we do not want its opposite: the kind of class in which we do most of the talking and supply most of the effort, struggling to drag and push the students through a mire.

Unfortunately, establishing the coordinated movement of "controlled drift" in the classroom isn't as simple as launching a canoe in a river, sitting back, and enjoying the ride. At the beginning of a course, the current and direction aren't already there except as an implicit hope, among teachers and students, for this kind of experience. Even if students and teachers share this hope, comfortable interaction rarely occurs immediately among strangers. In addition, conventional roles and expectations can inhibit this interaction. When you enter the classroom on the first day you will be the center of attention. Your students will defer to your authority and wait for you to speak — to tell them what the course will be like and what you expect them to do. They have no way of knowing what roles you want them to play, and their assumptions will not necessarily produce the kind of cohesive, interactive class you hope for. What you say at that point of departure, in class and on your syllabus, can determine what happens for the rest of the term.

> If you hope for a class that integrates writing and reading with lively discussion and student presentations, you have to adopt those goals from the beginning, when you design your course, and keep them in mind as you structure assignments and activities.

We have known many teachers who genuinely wanted this kind of class and felt disappointed when it didn't turn out that way; but they had nearly excluded the possibility from the beginning. They maintained one set of goals as vague hopes and used other goals to design their courses, around long, undifferentiated reading lists, disconnected writing assignments, and sequences of topics they had to cover each week. We cannot expect students to share responsibility for the class unless we give them this responsibility in our course designs. And we cannot expect them to participate extensively unless we structure occasions and allow ample time for this participation.

When we have used these goals to plan our courses, furthermore, we need to make these goals and plans explicit to our students in considerable detail. Many teachers seem to believe, in spite of evidence to the contrary, that undergraduates have psychic powers. Although the kinds of reading, writing, and student participation they expect from students are highly specialized, they treat these expectations as though they were universal or assume that good students will use mysterious powers of inference to figure out what the teacher wants. And undergraduates will often try to perform these feats of inference, rather than asking for clarification, because they are conditioned to believe that figuring out "what teachers really want" is the student's job. If they feel that their role in the course is to figure out what you want them to do, through trial and error, they will never reach the level of composure and trust that allows a class to move along in that wonderful way that is both lively and relaxed, with its own momentum.

9

Strategies for Including Writing in Large Courses

Key Elements

Enlarging Conceptions of Writing for Large Courses   147

Even in the largest classes, there are always ways in which students can write and interact productively, without making the class overwhelmingly time-consuming for you. When integrated with learning, even small amounts of writing can be of great benefit.

Assigning Less to Achieve More   149

Short papers and writing exercises usually work better in a large class, because they can be linked with instruction more directly and returned to students more promptly. Some examples include

- explanations of central or difficult concepts (1 paragraph to 1 page)
- writing exercises during or at the end of a lecture (1 page or a large note card)
- summaries of readings (1 page)
- short position papers (1–2 pages)
- research exercises (2–3 pages)
- research proposals (1–2 pages)

Assigning Writing That Is Not Graded (or Even Read)   150

The potential benefit of writing extends well beyond its use as an object of evaluation. When you consider ways of including writing in a large course, therefore, you should consider a variety of options concerning reading, response, and evaluation.

Responding to Writing: Taking Time to Save Time   153

Some methods that take time in order to save time:

- Save examples of student papers and of your comments to remind you of instructions you need to provide the next time you use the writing assignment.
- Save exceptionally good papers and get permission from the writers to distribute copies as models in future semesters.
- Watch for and make copies of published essays that you can use as models.
- When you produce writing assignments, pause to consider the kind of writing you hope to receive and describe those expectations in the assignment itself.
- When you receive a batch of student papers, begin by reading a number of them without comment, to observe general patterns or problems you can describe in a handout, and make a list of these patterns as you read.
- While you read and comment on individual papers, continue to add patterns you notice to the list, and comment only on the distinctive features of the paper at hand. Compose a handout to cover the common patterns.
- Save the lists and handouts for revising assignments and planning future versions of the course.

Making the Best Use of Discussion Sections and Teaching Assistants   154

- Discussion sections should have their own functions and learning goals, related to but contextually separate from the lectures.
- Discussion sections can include most of the writing and learning activities we have described in previous chapters, with due consideration for the limited time available.
- The professors should help design the discussion sections and should also train and supervise teaching assistants.
- Teaching assistants placed in charge of discussion sections both need and deserve training and supervision.
- If peer tutors trained by the writing center or other programs are assigned to a course, the professor should provide additional guidance specific to his or her course.
- Make sure that appropriate rooms are reserved for discussion sections.
- Do not exploit teaching assistants.

Offering Optional Sections or Assignments for Highly Motivated Students   156

In most classes, some students are deeply interested in the subject, have advanced knowledge, or would welcome more challenging assignments. In every field, we have found, some students would rather demonstrate their knowledge in writing and discussion than on formal examinations. Optional, writing-intensive sections and optional writing assignments can provide these alternatives without creating overwhelming amounts of work for the teacher.

Enlarging Conceptions of Writing for Large Courses

Classes devoted to writing instruction are typically small but often larger than their teachers would prefer. Asked about the ideal enrollment for a writing class, most composition teachers would suggest about fifteen students, even fewer for ESL or developmental courses that include frequent conferences. Reality doesn't often correspond with this ideal, but undergraduate writing classes always cap enrollments, at an average of about twenty students and often fewer. The reasons are fairly obvious. Like foreign language instruction, writing instruction requires attention to individual students, interaction among students and teachers, and extensive practice. If students are continually writing and revising papers, teachers must read, respond to, and evaluate this work, often in multiple drafts, and keep track of each student's progress. Teaching writing is therefore labor-intensive, as the consistently low enrollments in writing classes essentially prove. If there were viable ways to deliver this instruction to classes of one hundred students or more, many colleges and universities would have chosen this efficient option.

If you teach large classes, therefore, you might conclude that providing significant writing instruction is a lost cause, best left to writing professionals and other teachers of small courses. Faculty who genuinely want to improve student writing in their fields are often discouraged even from assigning papers in large courses, because they don't have time in these contexts to provide instructive guidance and feedback or to accommodate revisions — the most basic features of writing instruction. And the most dedicated teachers, in this regard, are often the most easily discouraged by weak writing they can't do much to improve.

As composition teachers in a program that limits writing seminars to seventeen students, we appreciate the luxury of teaching writing in small classes, and we can't pretend that we could give comparable attention to student writing in classes of thirty, fifty, or a hundred students or more. Like the sizes and designs of college courses, however, the kinds of writing practice and instruction that *are* possible occur on a continuum that includes many variables. Some of these variables, often including enrollments, are unalterable, but there are still many alternative ways of teaching within a course of a certain size, general design, and function within the curriculum. There is no point in wishing that a large course were really a small seminar. This wish, or regret, leads teachers to narrow their conceptions of writing and writing instruction to the assignment of formal essays and long research papers, graded and returned with extensive comments and suggestions for revision. And this conception leads them either to attempt the impossible or to do nothing with writing at all.

> We suggest that there are more and less effective ways of teaching courses of any particular size. And even in the largest classes, there are always ways in which students can write and interact productively, without making the class overwhelmingly time-consuming for the teacher.

Within limiting conditions, uses of language and forms of learning are also limited, but some limitations apply to any type of instruction, including a seminar. In a large course you won't be able to transform student writing in a single term, but teachers in small classes can rarely do so either. Students become effective writers through continual practice in a variety of circumstances. When integrated with learning, even small amounts of writing can be of great benefit.

Because so many variables other than numbers of students determine the types and amounts of writing you can assign in a course, we will not try to correlate this work with levels of enrollment. What you can accomplish in a class of eighty students, for example, will depend on the number of credit hours the course offers, the availability of teaching assistants at your school, and whether the course includes smaller discussion or lab sections. Along with other responsibilities, teaching loads vary considerably from one college to another and affect the amounts of time teachers can devote to specific courses. The functions of writing also differ among the disciplines and, within a discipline, among levels of instruction. What would seem possible and appropriate for one teacher of an eighty-student course can be impossible or inappropriate for another teacher at a different school, in a different field of study, or at another level of the curriculum.

As a consequence, we offer a variety of ideas and strategies for including writing in large classes and let you decide which will be most useful in the courses you teach. Some of these suggestions apply especially to classes with high enrollments. In other cases we have drawn from previous chapters methods that can work in courses of all sizes, including very large ones.

Assigning Less to Achieve More

In Chapter 8 we noted that teachers often falsely equate amounts of reading with amounts of learning or understanding of the material. This is one example of a broader notion that students will learn more if teachers assign more work. Another particularly questionable example is the assumption that students will learn more from writing a ten-page paper than they will from writing one or two pages.

When teachers complain that reading and grading papers consume too much of their time, we often find that they have assigned long essays or elaborate research papers without considering the goals and benefits of these assignments. Indeed, students must work hard to complete these papers, and teachers must work equally hard (or even harder in a large class) to read and evaluate the products of this labor. If the writers were pressed for time or were struggling to fill the page requirements, evaluating the poor results can be especially time-consuming and discouraging. And the idea that pain equals gain can mask the futility of these endeavors, by leaving both students and teachers with a grim sense of virtue for having completed a difficult, unpleasant task. The illusion of benefit is often just relief in disguise.

In appropriate circumstances, complex research projects and long essays can be valuable learning experiences, but a large class is rarely the appropriate context for these assignments. Without opportunities for class discussion and guidance in the process of writing, these assignments will seem disconnected from ongoing work in the course.

> Short papers and writing exercises usually work better in a large class because they can be linked with instruction more directly and returned to students more promptly.

Even a single paragraph can be a valuable learning exercise. Brief writing exercises keep you in touch with your students' understanding and confusion — a kind of attention increasingly difficult to maintain as enrollments rise. For busy teachers, there are obvious advantages in reading one paragraph or one page rather than several pages. In many cases the goals you want to meet in ambitious assignments, such as research papers, can be achieved more successfully in focused exercises.

The specific forms and purposes of small writing exercises vary greatly among courses, but here are some general types, with approximate lengths.

- *Explanations of central or difficult concepts* (1 paragraph to 1 page). Ask students to complete these assignments at home, with an emphasis on clear, concise explanation.

- *Writing exercises during or at the end of a lecture* (1 page or a large note card). To break the tedium of continuous lectures, pose a difficult question and ask students to respond in writing. These responses can substitute for discussion or question periods, in which participation is uneven in large courses, or they can be used to stimulate participation. At the end of class, leave a few minutes for students to summarize the lecture and raise questions. Collect this writing for your own reference, so you can address questions and misconceptions in the next class.

- *Summaries of readings* (1 page). These assignments, completed outside class, improve students' grasp of reading assignments and let you know how well they understood the material.

- *Short position papers* (1–2 pages). These assignments ask students to develop positions on central issues raised in lectures or readings and draw students in large classes into debate of these issues.

- *Research exercises* (2–3 pages). Teachers often assign large research papers to expose students to library or online resources, including primary literature. But you can meet many of these goals just as effectively by telling students to locate, summarize, and document two or three good sources on a focused topic.

- *Research proposals* (1–2 pages). Especially in advanced classes, students can begin to identify interesting research questions and develop methods for answering these questions. This exercise is comparable to the introduction and methods sections of a research article, and it can include a brief literature review in the introduction.

Assigning Writing That Is Not Graded (or Even Read)

The prospect of including writing in a large course seems especially daunting when teachers assume that they have to read, respond to, and grade all writing they assign. Students expect and deserve such attention to formal papers, and on other kinds of work they welcome whatever feedback you can provide. For some types of writing, however, grading is unnecessary or even inappropriate. Along with other kinds of informal writing or "writing to learn," some of the short writing exercises we described in the previous section should not be graded and do not require written comments. In some cases, such as responses to questions you ask in lectures, students can benefit more from exchanging and discussing their work in class.

The general principle we want to stress is that the potential benefits of writing extend well beyond its use as an object of evaluation. Everything students write does not have to pass through a system of exchange that converts its value ultimately to a grade. And if you have too many students and too little time, there are several levels of exchange from which you can choose.

When you consider ways of including writing in a large course, therefore, you should consider a variety of options concerning reading, response, and evaluation:

- *Writing you do not collect.* This option usually includes informal writing students do in class or writing they bring to class (such as study questions or paper topics) for exchange and discussion with one another.

- *Writing you collect and read briefly but do not grade.* This category might include informal writing produced in or outside class, used to stimulate thinking, guide reading, and tell you how well students understand the subject.

- *Writing you collect, read briefly, and acknowledge for credit.* When teachers want to make sure that students take writing exercises or short papers (such as summaries of readings) seriously, they often simply note whether the work meets minimum standards and include that credit in the final grade. This practice is often used for course journals or writing notebooks that teachers collect periodically and return, with or without comments.

- *Writing you read, with a few comments, and grade with an alternative system.* For informal papers, exercises, or drafts, teachers often use check systems or other ways of indicating an approximate level of quality, without assigning formal letter or numerical grades. The most common system uses a ✓ to indicate satisfactory work, a ✓+ for exceptionally good work, and a ✓− for poor work. These marks are then collectively averaged into the final grade for the course. But there are many other possible systems. In an advanced geometry class that includes constant writing and revision for solving problems, David Henderson marks student work with portions of a circle to indicate the extent to which students have approached a complete understanding of the problem.

- *Writing you read with extensive comments but do not grade.* This practice is especially useful for short proposals, introductions, and other work students submit early in the process of developing longer papers, when thoughtful advice can have the greatest benefit.

- *Finished papers you evaluate with comments and grades.* Comments on finished, formal assignments do not have to be extensive, but they should provide a clear, substantial assessment of the strengths and weaknesses of the paper and clear support for the grade.

It is especially important for you to explain these choices to your students when you give them writing assignments and exercises.

Because they are also very busy, your students will understand that you have limited time to devote to their work. They most often feel disappointed or short-changed when they expect to receive grades or detailed comments and do not. You can avoid most of this disappointment by telling students in advance, for each type of assignment, what they can expect from you in feedback and evaluation and why you have made these decisions. For example, if you tell students that you will have time only to make two or three general observations at the end of each paper, they will not expect detailed comments in the margins. And if you explain that you cannot mark and correct specific errors, your students will not assume that clean pages mean their writing is flawless.

Example

In Chapter 1 we described some very effective assignments that economist Robert Frank developed for economics majors in a fairly small, advanced class. The assignments asked students to observe, think, and write as "economic naturalists": "to use a principle, or principles, discussed in the course to explain some pattern of events or behavior you personally have observed."

Frank considered this application of principles to empirical phenomena so important that he adapted the economic naturalist assignments to an introductory microeconomics course with more than four hundred students and developed a new system for reading and grading these assignments. He limited the length of each of the two papers to 750 words and asked his teaching assistants to read them very quickly, grading them only with a check system to indicate whether they fulfilled the purpose of the assignment. Each teaching assistant also looked for exceptionally good papers and selected ten to receive bonus points. Frank read these selected papers and chose twenty of the best ones to receive additional bonus points.

Because he wants to give students the opportunity to read one another's work, Frank is currently experimenting with a peer-grading system. Students submit papers electronically, identified only by their ID numbers. TAs distribute five of these papers electronically to each student in the class and ask them to rank the papers from 1 to 5. The top 10 to 20% of these papers are posted on the course Web site, and students are asked to nominate the ten best. About forty of the top-scoring papers receive bonus points, and Frank chooses twenty of these to receive further points. This system engages students in the evaluation process, provides models and further learning from numerous examples, and creates considerable motivation for writing well.

Responding to Writing: Taking Time to Save Time

Treating each paper as a unique literary object gives students personal attention they appreciate, but this kind of attention isn't always possible. Nor is it always most effective. Even in small seminars, we often find ourselves saying the same things in our comments to several students — sometimes to the majority. And when we have finished reading a batch of papers, we often wish we had anticipated common problems, with clearer instructions for writing. In a small class we can absorb repetition and regret as reasonable costs of individualized instruction. In large classes these become intolerable costs that make attention to student writing tedious, inefficient, or even impossible.

In classes of any size, repetition and regret result from observing patterns and problems too late in the process of assigning, reading, and responding to student work. When we finish grading each paper before going on to the next, we gradually identify common patterns among them, through the repetition of our comments. By that time, a list of general comments for everyone seems redundant, because we have already said these things to a number of individual students. So we continue as we began, trying to find different language to deliver the same messages. Delayed reaction also explains many of those regrets about advice that we should have delivered in the assignment itself. We can't anticipate all the problems students will encounter when they complete our assignments, but teachers often compose writing assignments without stopping to think in advance about the kinds of papers they hope to receive. Taking the time at the beginning to make these expectations clear can save lots of time and disappointment later.

In other words, inefficiency usually results from an expedient effort to be efficient. If you are really busy, you want to get right to work on the task at hand. If you have an assignment to write, you want to get it written as quickly as possible. If you have a large stack of papers to read and grade, you want to get each one done before you go on to the next, to make the remaining pile smaller. Finding more efficient methods therefore requires pausing to think ahead or to look back.

Some methods that take time in order to save time:

- Save examples of student papers and of your comments to remind you of instructions you need to provide the next time you use the writing assignment.

- Save exceptionally good student papers that represent the kind of writing you want students to produce, and get permission from the writers to distribute copies as models in future semesters. Exceptionally good responses to your assignment can help to clarify your standards, expectations, and evaluations. In some ways, students will get a more complete, detailed sense of the kind of writing you admire from these examples than they will from specific comments on their own papers.

- Watch for and make copies of published essays (your own included) that you can use as models.

- When you produce writing assignments, pause to consider the kind of writing you hope to receive and describe those expectations in the assignment itself.

- When you receive a batch of student papers, begin by reading a number of them without comment, to observe general patterns or problems you can describe in a handout, and make a list of these patterns as you read.

- While you read and comment on individual papers, continue to add patterns you notice to the list, and comment only on the distinctive features of the paper at hand. Compose a handout to cover the common patterns.

- Save the lists and handouts for revising assignments and planning future versions of the course.

Making the Best Use of Discussion Sections and Teaching Assistants

In large classes, discussion sections and teaching assistants are often underutilized, even wasted resources. Lost opportunities usually result from the tendency of professors to think of the lectures, assigned readings, and exams as the core of their courses. Discussion sections therefore appear to have limited functions, primarily to review material students missed or misunderstood or to help them prepare for exams. Teaching assistants, in turn, become graders and leaders of "review sessions." Their main jobs are to evaluate student work and to clarify, in discussion sections or in conferences, what professors and assigned texts have already said.

These functions waste potential resources: discussion sections can enrich a large course with many of the benefits of small seminars, including lively discussion, other kinds of active and interactive learning, and related attention to writing. Because teaching assistants usually have more direct contact with the students than the professor does,
can engage students in many kinds of learning that are impos-
to provide in lectures. Graduate and undergraduate teaching as-
nts who will become educators also need to develop effective teach-
skills in positions of acknowledged responsibility, with the training
supervision necessary to help them teach effectively. They receive
of these benefits from jobs as graders or as monitors of review
sions.

We realize that these resources vary considerably among colleges
nd universities, so we cannot describe a typical circumstance. Not all
arge classes include discussion sections. At undergraduate colleges
without graduate programs, professors often lead discussion sections
in their own courses, without help from teaching assistants. Some of

these schools employ undergraduate teaching assistants or peer tutors to lead discussion or laboratory sections or to work individually with students in a course. Writing centers sometimes train undergraduate peer tutors specifically to help students with writing assignments in particular courses. Graduate programs also vary greatly in scale and relation to undergraduate studies, and different schools place varying restrictions on the roles of graduate teaching assistants in the classroom. Some are allowed to teach virtually autonomous courses, under the supervision of faculty. Others are not allowed even to grade student work.

Any general advice we offer will therefore raise many exceptions, and we will limit our suggestions to a few basic principles:

- Whether they are led by professors or teaching assistants, discussion sections should have their own functions and learning goals, related to but contextually separate from the lectures. Activities and assignments in the sections should be planned in advance, like other features of the course, not left to chance.

- Because they are small classes within larger ones, discussion sections can include most of the writing and learning activities we have described in previous chapters, with due consideration for the limited time available. These activities include many kinds of informal writing, discussion of plans and drafts for formal papers, peer review, other work in small groups, debates, field studies, presentations, and poster sessions.

- The professors who lead such courses are primarily responsible for whatever occurs in discussion sections. If they do not lead these sections, they should help design them. They should also train and supervise teaching assistants.

- Teaching assistants placed in charge of discussion sections both need and deserve training and supervision in planning and leading classroom activities, evaluating and commenting on student work, holding conferences with students, and any other responsibilities they are assigned.

- If peer tutors trained by the writing center or other programs are assigned to a course, the professor should provide additional guidance specific to his or her course. If peer tutors are supposed to work with students on writing assignments, for example, the professors should make the purpose, form, and standards for these assignments clear to the tutors. Even the most talented and well-trained tutors cannot fully anticipate these expectations, especially if they are majors in a different field of study.

- Make sure that appropriate rooms are reserved for discussion sections. These sections are often limited to the functions of question and answer periods by the structures of the rooms, with fixed seating in rows facing a lectern. Without saws and wrenches, it is almost impossible to convert such rooms to the purposes of interactive learning and close attention to writing.

While discussion sections led by teaching assistants can greatly enrich a large course, with writing and learning activities characteristic of a seminar, these uses of the section periods should not lead to the exploitation of teaching assistants as a labor force. One of the main responsibilities of professors, in fact, is to make sure that workloads for teaching assistants do not exceed the time for which they are paid to teach and that individual teaching assistants do not become victims of duty. Training and supervision should include monitoring the time required to lead the sections effectively, along with efficient methods for completing this work. Many of the suggestions we have made for responding to student papers and leading classroom activities can support this training.

Offering Optional Sections or Assignments for Highly Motivated Students

For convenience, we tend to think of the students in a large class as a homogeneous mass and assume that real differences in their ability or motivation will sort out in examinations and other general requirements. In most of these classes, however, some students are deeply interested in the subject, have advanced knowledge, or would welcome more challenging assignments, while others are content to meet the minimum requirements. Undergraduates also differ in their preferred forms of learning and performance. In every field, we have found, some students would rather demonstrate their knowledge in writing and discussion than on formal examinations. These students often feel disadvantaged and discouraged by the overall structure of the class.

Optional Weekly or Biweekly Sections

For these reasons, many large courses affiliated with the Writing in the Majors Program at Cornell offer optional weekly or biweekly sections in which students learn the course material through writing, discussion, debates, field studies, and other activities. These sections, led by advanced graduate students in the discipline, usually carry one additional credit, and the students enrolled in these sections typically do not take the regular examinations in the course. Optional sections are listed in the course catalog, and students request admission to the sections on forms they complete at the beginning of the term, with explanations of their reasons for choosing the option.

These optional sections with different requirements can be offered regardless of whether the course includes weekly discussion sections. If there are regularly scheduled sections for all students in the course, the optional sections still differ in design and purpose, carry an additional credit, and sometimes meet twice each week rather than once.

We have worked with two successful courses that have three tiers: a basic lecture course without sections, the lecture course with discussion sections each week, and a writing-intensive section for the more highly motivated students in the class. In all of these variations, optional sections allow teachers of large classes to offer writing, lively discussion, and other opportunities to the students who are most interested in these challenges, without adding overwhelming amounts of work to their teaching loads.

Optional Writing Assignments

For similar reasons, teachers often offer optional writing assignments or revisions to interested students, with or without extra credit. In some cases these options replace examinations, or the grades on the papers can replace examination grades if they are higher. These choices are most appealing to students who have special interest in the subject or to those who prefer writing essays to taking examinations. In many cases the options include a research paper. Professors who would like to assign research projects but cannot face the large number of papers they would have to read can therefore make this opportunity available to the relatively small number of students who will choose it.

We should note, however, that the students who choose to write research papers will not necessarily know how to complete such projects effectively. The advice we offer about research-based assignments in Chapter 7 applies as much to optional research papers as to general requirements. If you offer this choice, in other words, you should take responsibility for providing guidance in the process of research and writing and should not just collect the finished products at the end of the term.

Assigning Group Projects

If you have a large number of students enrolled in your class, the mathematical advantage of group projects is fairly obvious, though somewhat deceptive. If one hundred students are working in teams of four, you will have only twenty-five reports or papers to read rather than one hundred. Team presentations, in turn, will require considerably less class time than individual presentations. Because most of the professions students enter require teamwork, including reports and presentations, these projects also offer kinds of learning that are often neglected in undergraduate studies, which emphasize individual, competitive performance.

Because these skills are neglected, however, many students have not learned how to work effectively in teams — in research, in writing, or in presentations — and you will need to take some responsibility for teaching and monitoring these activities. We have heard many tales of conflict, frustration, and injustice from participants in groups that were left to their own devices in these projects. Without clear guidance and organization, undergraduates can have difficulty establishing roles and distributing work evenly. Some members will assume too much responsibility; others will assume too little; and if the results are disappointing, the members of the team will blame one another. For these reasons and others, group projects can become very negative learning experiences that teach participants to avoid collaboration.

As a consequence, if you assign group projects, simple division will not yield an entirely accurate savings of time and attention, but the educational benefits and some of the time-saving advantages remain. Ideally, you should meet with each group to establish goals and methods toward the beginning of the project, and you should check in with the groups later to make sure the work is progressing smoothly and fairly. In large classes, it is sometimes impossible to provide this individual attention, but you can avoid most of the potential problems through general guidelines and other efficient ways of monitoring collaborative work.

Personality differences and disagreements are in fact normal features of collaboration, and you can't expect to eliminate these challenges altogether. Instead, you need to provide methods for resolving potential conflicts — methods that students will not be able to invent reliably on their own. The following suggestions include methods of accounting for and evaluating individual participation, because students will tend to work together more effectively if they know their own performance will count in the end.

Guidelines for Group Projects

- When you assign group projects, provide clear methods for establishing roles and distributing labor, along with timetables for the completion of stages in the process and specifications for the finished product.

- Using a written assignment, a survey, or a class discussion, ask students to describe the kind of team member they would prefer to work with, and make the results known to the class. With this awareness, most students will want to become the type of participant they and their peers prefer.

- Announce that you are available to help resolve any problems that arise during the project, including disagreements among members or individual dissatisfaction.

- When the project is well under way, schedule some class time for discussion of difficulties in research, writing, or group dynamics.

- In collaborative writing projects, ask each team to submit a page that describes the division of labor: who did what and how the finished report or paper came about.

- Use what some teachers call "social grades" for evaluation of individual performance in the project, as a portion of each student's final grade. In these systems, members of the team evaluate everyone's contributions to the project, including their own, with numerical or letter grades, accompanied by brief explanations. While such evaluations are unusual in undergraduate studies, they are common features of performance reviews in professions.

Example

In a senior computer science course on software design, Bard Bloom assigned all design projects to varying teams of four students in a class of one hundred. At the end of each project, all team members were given 40 points to distribute among the members, including themselves, according to the quality of their contributions. They also submitted brief written explanations of their criteria for these distributions. In addition, at the end of the term students could nominate others who were especially good team members for special commendations that carried a large number of extra points.

In Chapter 8, we recommended guidelines for oral presentations, including team presentations on group projects. Here we will simply add that while a group presentation requires more class time than an individual presentation, well-organized team presentations are still considerably more efficient in large classes. Clear time limits and guidelines should force the groups to develop efficient plans and individual roles in the performance.

Using Writing Centers to Help with Instruction

Most colleges and universities now have some type of writing center that provides instructional support for faculty and students, and these centers can be especially useful to teachers who assign writing in large classes. Because the functions of writing centers vary considerably, we first encourage you to find out what services are available at your school.

Here are some of the most common features that writing centers offer:

- Individual consultation and workshops for faculty, for help with writing assignments, writing instruction, and evaluation of papers

- Individual tutoring services for students who need help with a particular writing assignment or particular writing difficulties, including ESL problems

- Developmental courses or workshops for students who need special writing instruction

- Instructional materials on writing for distribution to your students

- Trained peer tutors who can be assigned to specific courses or students

- Libraries of reference books on writing instruction, teaching materials, and pedagogy

If you recommend that individual students visit the writing center, you should note that these are not proofreading or correction services. Peer tutors and other staff are trained to help students identify, understand, and take responsibility for weaknesses in their own writing, not to edit or rewrite papers for the students. In this way and others, writing centers offer *instructional* support, to teachers and to students, and this is the kind of help you should expect from them. They will not simply clean up your students' papers. Instead, they will help you assign and respond to student writing more effectively, and they can help address student writing problems you do not have time to address in a large class.

The Transforming Power of Words

In his classic work *Pedagogy of the Oppressed*, the Brazilian educator Paulo Freire observes, "The outstanding characteristic of . . . narrative education . . . is the sonority of words, not their transforming power" (57). Narrative education, in Freire's view, casts the teacher as the "narrating Subject" and the students as "patient, listening objects," vessels to be filled with knowledge. Students in this position, he says, are not really authorized or taught to think, because "authentic thinking, thinking that is concerned about *reality*, does not take place in ivory tower isolation, but only in communication" (64). If contexts for learning discourage students from communicating their thoughts, in writing or in speech, education will transform neither the learners nor the world in which they live. Due to the prevalence of narrative education throughout the world, Freire concludes that "education is suffering from narration sickness" (57).

While the conventional academic lecture epitomizes the features of "narrative education," the teachers we know who "narrate" the content of their courses to large numbers of students are not deliberate agents of oppression, intent on lulling undergraduates into submission through the "sonority of words." Most of these teachers believe, like Freire, that language and learning should have "transforming power." Through lectures and assigned readings they hope to convey knowledge and ideas that will change the ways in which students think and act in the world. And this hope persists in part because the most dynamic, compelling speakers *can* sometimes affect their audiences in these ways. Every college or university faculty includes professors known for their exciting, inspiring lectures, and traditions of fine teaching in higher education are primarily traditions of brilliant narration.

These traditions are most compelling for teachers of large classes and are built into the structures of the lecture halls assigned to these courses: with fixed seating in rows, facing a stage on which teachers are expected to perform. The descending rows of seats in an auditorium contribute to this assumption that the teacher will be the center of attention, easily seen and heard by students who watch and listen but cannot easily speak to or hear one another. If fine teaching is brilliant narration — an engaging story about the topic — contributions from the audience will seem like interruptions. Exchanges among students will be disruptive. In such contexts the most "natural" recourse is to speak continuously and make the lecture as clear and interesting as you can.

"Narration" certainly has useful functions in higher education, for conveying information clearly and coherently to large numbers of students, and it isn't possible to maintain lively, inclusive discussions, like those in a small seminar, with groups of 50 or 150 people. Periodic discussions in pairs or small groups will allow students to exchange ideas and learn from one another and will relieve the tedium of unbroken lectures. If your class isn't too large, you can use group presentations to invert roles and place students on the stage, with active responsibility for the class. Unlike question periods, usually dominated by a few vocal students, these activities include everyone.

In large courses, however, writing is the most flexible, useful medium for including students in active communication, in ways that enrich learning. Brief writing exercises during and after lectures give students time to digest course material and raise questions. If you collect this writing you will understand more fully what students are learning and thinking; and if you discuss their ideas and questions in the next class, students will have active voices in the substance of the course. Informal writing they complete at home can have similar functions. Short papers of various kinds improve reading comprehension, give students opportunities to formulate and convey positions on central issues, grasp important concepts, or pursue their own research questions.

Such writing can have "transforming power" for you and for your students, because it will change the nature and quality of learning in your course.

10

Teaching as a Work in Progress

Key Elements

A Course as a Work in Progress   163

Like a complex writing project, a course is always to some extent a work in progress. A syllabus is really just an outline for a course that has yet to be composed in the practice of teaching, from one week to the next.

In itself, of course, structure is not an impediment to change; nor does an improvisational approach necessarily yield the kinds of revision that improve teaching.

Learning from Experience: Record Keeping   164

Regardless of the extent to which you make and follow plans, another variable can have profound effects on the development of courses and teaching careers. This variable is the extent to which you pay attention to, record, and learn from your teaching experience.

If we return to the conception of teaching as a kind of research, records of teaching seem equally essential, both to improve courses and to establish credentials for teaching careers.

Methods for developing records of teaching:

- Maintain complete, orderly files of teaching materials.
- Save examples of student writing and your comments.
- Maintain a teaching journal.
- Invite colleagues to visit and evaluate your classes.
- Develop a teaching portfolio.

A Course as a Work in Progress

In the first chapter of this book, we encouraged a view of teaching as a kind of research: an ongoing investigation into the ways in which students learn a subject. Course design thus resembles research design, based on hypotheses about learning that we test, and often revise, as the term progresses. In this investigation, student writing, discussion, and course evaluations provide evidence of student responses to our teaching strategies: data we can use to revise our plans in this or the next version of a course.

There are equally strong parallels between teaching and writing.

> Like a complex writing project, a course is always to some extent a work in progress.

A detailed syllabus, like a table of contents, appears to describe a course that is already fully composed, at least in the teacher's mind, and we often talk about our courses in this fashion, as though they were completed texts we can repeat the following year. Unless it describes a scripted monologue, however, a syllabus is really just an outline for a course that has yet to be composed in the practice of teaching, from one week to the next. And in the following year, even if the syllabus remains the same, the course will no doubt change. From one year to another, new students enter our classes, with different backgrounds, motivations, and interests in the subject. The functions of a course within the curriculum gradually shift as well, along with the significance of its topics and readings. Our teaching practices also change on the basis of past experience, even if we follow the same plans. If the reality of a course resides in the classroom, therefore, we never teach the same course twice. Instead, each rendition becomes a draft for the next. Perhaps the main difference between teaching and writing is that a teaching project is never really finished, only discontinued. To the extent that poems and other texts are never finished, as the cliché tells us, but only abandoned, perhaps teaching and writing projects share that similarity as well.

Like writers, furthermore, teachers make and follow plans to varying degrees. Some prepare detailed outlines that they follow closely, because they feel they need this structure to avoid getting lost in the process. Such teachers usually revise their courses between terms, just as such writers usually revise complete drafts. Other teachers and writers need only a few notes and ideas before they plunge into the endeavor in an exploratory fashion, continually improvising and revising as they proceed.

These opposites and the variations between them seem to be matters of individual preference and context. Because we've observed that all of these variations can produce good teaching or bad teaching (and good writing or bad writing), we can't prescribe an approach that everyone should use. In specific cases, it's true that too much structure or too little structure can interfere with teaching. All of us need to find our own point of balance between rigid adherence to plans and insufficient preparation. In itself, however, structure is not an impediment to change; nor does an improvisational approach necessarily yield the kinds of revision that improve teaching.

Learning from Experience: Record Keeping

Another variable, however, can have profound effects on the development of courses and teaching careers, regardless of how we make and follow plans. This variable is the extent to which we pay attention to, record, and learn from teaching experience.

If highly structured courses become brittle with age, or if exploratory approaches lead nowhere, teachers have usually failed to register and make use of information that could improve their courses. Some of that information is readily available in the day-to-day experiences of teaching, including student writing and participation, and in the ideas that occur about that experience. Why did a particular class go well or poorly? Which strategies should we use again, avoid repeating, or revise? As we rush from one responsibility to another, we often forget even to ask such questions, much less to answer them in forms we can recall a week or a year later. Other kinds of information we need to elicit from students — in course evaluations, informal writing, and conferences — or find in references and resource centers for teachers. And having gathered this information, we need to refer to it when we make plans for teaching again, or the previous version of the course will tend to resurrect itself by default, like an old draft the writer can't move beyond.

If we return to the conception of teaching as a kind of research, records of teaching seem equally essential, both to improve courses and to establish credentials for teaching careers. Research would be pointless if we didn't bother to record and interpret the results. Yet scholars who keep meticulous records of their research activity often maintain only sketchy documentation of their teaching, confined to copies of syllabi, assignments, and final evaluations. This material provides an incomplete, unreliable basis for describing, revising, and assessing teaching methods.

Poor record keeping is especially unfortunate for new teachers, who will probably need to demonstrate teaching methods and skills for job searches and reviews. Graduate students who are immersed in specialized research often view teaching undergraduates primarily as a means of supporting this research. As a consequence, they underestimate the importance of teaching ability and experience in their future searches for academic jobs, often at schools where undergraduate education is the highest priority. Asked to submit statements of their teaching philosophy and sample materials, they have little to offer, even if they taught extensively and effectively. Similar problems can arise for faculty members who face tenure review or apply for jobs at different schools that place greater emphasis on teaching and on the teaching of writing in undergraduate studies.

The advice we offer here therefore serves related purposes: the revision and improvement of teaching, and the development of strong teaching credentials.

- *Maintain complete, orderly files of teaching materials.* It's difficult to revise or to describe your teaching methods if you haven't saved your material, can't find it, or can't make sense of what you've found. While you are teaching, you should at least keep all of the material you've used — syllabus, assignments, handouts, lists of readings, notes on classroom activities, student evaluations, and other documents — in a single place. Teachers often use paper folders, ring binders, or folders of computer files for this purpose. At the end of the term, when your memory is fresh, you should sort through this material and put it in some kind of order, so you can locate information, observe the structure of the course, and submit teaching material later, without having to sift through jumbled piles of information.

- *Save examples of student writing and your comments.* During the term, save some examples of the student writing that resulted from your assignments, along with your comments on that work. These can be examples of informal writing you found useful in your teaching, of papers that illustrate specific problems, or examples of especially good writing you could submit (with your comments) as evidence of your teaching skills. If you consider using student papers for the latter purpose or for other kinds of distribution, request the writers' permission.

- *Maintain a teaching journal.* Even if you save all of your course materials in orderly files, you won't recall what actually occurred and what you were thinking at the time unless you keep an ongoing record. Teaching journals, like the reflective journals we ask students to keep, also stimulate creative thinking of great value in revising courses. Some of the most brilliant ideas you have during the term will be lost if you don't write them down where you can find and use them later. We therefore recommend that you take a few minutes after each class, or at least at the end of each week, to write entries in a separate notebook or computer document reserved for this purpose, like a research notebook. Include "afterthoughts" on what worked, what didn't, what needs to happen next, how you would revise an assignment for future use, what readings need to be changed, and so on. You can use this journal to record spontaneous ideas you have at other times as well. This is also a good place to record summaries of what you learned from student evaluations, which will make less sense a year later. In addition, teaching journals are a good source of ideas for composing teaching philosophies, required in most applications for teaching positions.

- *Invite colleagues to visit and evaluate your classes.* In most colleges and universities, teaching is a rather private activity, and unless your department requires observation of your teaching, other teachers will rarely ask if they may attend one of your classes. Inviting them to visit can give you useful feedback on your methods. Written evaluations based on these visits can also provide valuable records of your teaching skills for job searches and reviews.

- *Develop a teaching portfolio.* If you apply for a teaching position or face review for reappointment, tenure, or promotion, you will probably need to submit a teaching portfolio that includes course materials, a statement of teaching philosophy and development, and evaluations of your teaching. It makes sense for you to have much of that material ready in advance if you want to present it well, rather than frantically trying to assemble it when the need arises. If you have a teaching portfolio on hand, you can selectively add the most useful material each term, including explanations for course designs and assignments. An effective teaching portfolio should clearly demonstrate not only what you taught, but also how you taught, why you chose those methods, how your strategies developed over time, and how well they worked.

These methods for keeping track of your teaching are especially important in writing and writing-intensive courses, partly because writing and related activities will complicate the tasks of understanding and describing what is going on in a course. If you were simply lecturing each class period to a passive audience of students who took periodic exams on this material, your syllabus, lecture notes, and final evaluations would provide a more or less complete record of what happened — or, in any case, all of the information readily available. In the kinds of instruction we describe in this book, an accurate record of what is going on in a course becomes much richer and more complex. When students are writing and speaking, interacting with one another and with their teachers, and sharing responsibility for the quality of the class, many sources of information become both available and essential to the development and assessment of teaching. This is why writing teachers, and teachers of language more generally, have been especially interested in pedagogy.

If you pursue a career as a writing teacher, therefore, all of these sources of information about your teaching will be vitally important and will be required in job applications and reviews. If you teach writing or writing-intensive courses in a field of study such as history, philosophy, biology, or psychology, this experience can also add exceptional value to your teaching credentials and career, especially if you are applying for positions in disciplines outside the traditional domains of writing instruction. Because many schools now have "writing across the curriculum" programs and requirements, academic departments are often especially interested in candidates who know how to teach writing in their fields of study. Many other schools are deeply concerned about the communication skills of their students and appreciate job applicants who are both aware of and have developed methods for meeting these needs.

More generally, teachers who include writing and other active uses of language in their courses tend to have more complex and interesting things to say about teaching and learning. Beyond their ability to teach writing, therefore, they can more easily demonstrate that they are thoughtful, professional teachers, aware of effective methods for engaging students in their fields of inquiry. On this point we return to Richard Light's conclusion from his studies at Harvard, which we cited in Chapter 8. Students appreciate language classes, Light argues, for the more general reason that they "are enthusiastic when classes are structured to maximize personal engagement and collegial interaction" (80). To the extent that writing instruction serves these purposes, learning to teach writing well is also a process of becoming a good teacher.

CONCLUSION

National Implications, Local Practices

W hile we were completing revisions of this book, in the spring of 2003, two events coincidentally shed some light, from very different directions, on the potential value of *The Elements of Teaching Writing* for college teachers and their students.

The first of these events was the launch of a broad campaign to increase and enrich writing instruction in American education. In April 2003, the National Commission on Writing in America's Schools and Colleges, sponsored by the College Board, released its report called "The Neglected 'R': The Need for a Writing Revolution." As the title of this report suggests, the commission found that writing has been seriously neglected in comparison with reading, mathematics, the sciences, and other important areas of instruction. In response, the commission recommends that the time students spend writing should be doubled over the next five years in all courses and subjects and at all levels of education, including college. Because the full text of this forty-page report is available at the NCW Web site (http://www.writingcommission.org), we will mention just a few of its most important proposals and implications for college teachers.

According to the commission, writing and associated thinking skills are neglected in our schools for two related reasons. One is that educators tend to define and measure "learning improvement" in terms of "facts, discrete areas of curriculum, and educational institutions" rather than the more interdisciplinary "ability of students to think, reason, and communicate." In addition, the commission found, "writing is a prisoner of time," for teachers and for students. Finding time for writing is especially difficult in secondary schools, where instructors responsible for more than one hundred students each day are "overwhelmed with the challenge of reading, responding to, and evaluating" even one-page papers each week. The assignment of longer work, such as research papers, has become increasingly rare. And this lack of experience with complex writing and thinking tasks in high school contributes to the litany of complaints from college teachers that we listed in our introduction. In the work of the average college freshman, errors are common, and "analyzing and synthesizing information are also beyond the scope of most first-year students. . . ."

Unlike many earlier cries of alarm over literacy crises, however, the commission does not blame high school English teachers or call for a resurrection of virtue in the "basics" of English grammar and composition. Like *The Elements of Teaching Writing*, the commission's report advocates the integration of writing instruction with learning in all fields of study, including the sciences and mathematics, and at all levels of education. Embracing principles of writing across the curriculum, the commission argues that "the concept of doubling writing time is feasible because of the near-total neglect of writing outside English departments. In history, foreign languages, mathematics, home economics, science, physical education, art, and social science, all students can be encouraged to write more — and to write more effectively."

Most important from the commission's perspective, however, is that making writing "a fundamental organizing objective of education" will help students to learn and think more effectively. A few quotations from "The Neglected 'R'" will illustrate its close correspondence with our arguments that writing and other active uses of language can greatly enrich learning in any field of study:

- "Writing is how students connect the dots in their knowledge."

- "If students are to make knowledge their own, they must struggle with the details, wrestle with the facts, and rework raw information and dimly understood concepts into language they can communicate to someone else."

- "Writing is not simply a way for students to demonstrate what they know. It is a way to help them understand what they know. At its best, writing is learning."

- "Writing is everybody's business, and state and local curriculum guidelines should require writing in every curriculum area and at all levels."

- "Teachers need to understand writing as a complex (and enjoyable) form of learning and discovery, both for themselves and for their students. Faculty in all disciplines should have access to professional development opportunities to help them improve student writing."

This ambitious distribution of responsibility for writing instruction will of course require the distribution of skills and strategies as well, among teachers who have little or no experience with writing in their classes. Toward this end, the commission calls upon professional writing teachers to share their knowledge with colleagues in other fields, and it recommends required workshops on writing instruction for teacher certification and for all faculty in higher education. In addition, the report offers a list of suggestions for the development of "learning communities" in which teachers freely exchange ideas and solve problems. The suggestions acknowledge that greater attention to writing means that teachers will need to learn how to teach in new ways, with new challenges and innovative methods they can best learn from one another, informally and in faculty development programs.

The work of this commission was motivated in part by recognition that the priorities of our educational systems, from primary school through college, are at odds with the demands and values of what college students call the "real world." The emphases on mathematics and science, factual and technical knowledge, have resulted from technological revolutions that seem to diminish the importance of the humanities, where writing and other communication skills were traditionally taught. But these revolutions have instead *increased* the demand for strong communication skills in most professions. The commission's report notes that "more than 90 percent of midcareer professionals recently cited the 'need to write effectively' as a skill 'of great importance' in their day-to-day work."

These demands from the "real world" have often been leveled directly at the College Board, which sponsored the National Commission on Writing, and this affiliation will influence the future of the commission's proposals. In its role as a gatekeeper for admissions and placement at all levels of education, the College Board has helped create the educational policies, teaching priorities, and curricula that its commission now proposes to revolutionize, through "a cultural sea change that would provide writing with sufficient time and resources in the classroom." It is not a coincidence that the College Board's sudden concern about writing proficiency immediately follows its decision to include writing assessment in the 2005 SAT. Similar changes will occur for the ACT and the GRE, which will affect undergraduate preparations for graduate studies. While preparing to assess complex skills in writing and critical thinking, the College Board had good reasons to worry that these skills were not being taught.

We expect that changes in testing alone will make writing a higher priority in American schools and colleges, and the kinds of instruction we describe in *The Elements of Teaching Writing* will become increasingly common. College and university administrators have already begun to call for the development and expansion of writing in the disciplines, presenting faculty members and academic departments with the challenge of figuring out how to teach writing without sacrificing the learning objectives and "content" of their courses. We hope that *The*

Elements of Teaching Writing will provide models and approaches that lead to the enrichment of learning in these fields.

The second event illustrates this hope and possibility, on the more modest scale at which our book was inspired.

A couple of days after we read the National Commission report, one of us attended a three-hour "symposium" initiated by the students in Rebecca Safran's writing-intensive sections of an evolutionary biology course. Safran's students wanted to hold this event to share the results of their individual research projects on specific issues in evolution. These projects had already been peer-reviewed, revised, and submitted as literature review papers in the class. This symposium was scheduled during the dreaded Finals Week, when all of these students were extremely busy. The elaborate PowerPoint presentations most of these students had carefully composed and rehearsed were not graded, and no one was required to attend.

Yet nearly all of Safran's students were there, speaking before a large, attentive audience of classmates, friends, teachers, and (in a couple of cases) family members on topics such as the function of aging, the origins of mitochondria, the evolution of feathers, and sexual cannibalism among arachnids. Each of them was, for ten minutes, an authority and teacher and then resumed the role of attentive learner and listener, asking sharply focused questions as time permitted.

This was a fitting culmination of a semester in which these students had grown accustomed to the lively exchange of ideas and information, through writing and discussion. With their teacher, they had formed "learning communities" of their own, and they did not want to disperse, at the end of the term, without sharing the results of their research projects as well. In addition, many of these sophomores and juniors had never given formal presentations, and they knew that this experience would be valuable in their graduate studies and careers.

Although our writing program had been involved with the development of this course for some years, for this symposium we directly provided only the refreshments and a member of the audience. Rebecca Safran contributed the superb organization (including a formal printed program) and the fine teaching that inspired the event. For this symposium, the motivation and effort, the teaching and learning experiences, and the enthusiasm all came from the students themselves.

This symposium, the course that preceded it, and many others we have observed embody the ideals we kept in mind as we completed *The Elements of Teaching Writing* and supplied most of the ideas we offer as well. We believe that this symposium and the course that led to it also embody the ideals and goals of the National Commission on Writing, at the level at which this campaign will actually succeed or fail. Summarizing the views of "educators and policy makers" in a *New York Times* article on "The Neglected 'R'" (26 Apr. 2003), Tamar Lewin concluded that the success or failure of the commission's proposals will depend on "national will."

Regardless of its fate at the level of national policy, national and state funding, or institutional mandates, these proposals will fail if teachers view writing as an instructional burden they must bear or as a distraction from real learning in their disciplines. In practice, revolutions in writing and learning do not occur on a national scale or result from national will. They occur in particular schools and classes, through the concerns, commitments, and ingenuity of individual teachers, and through the lively, willing participation of their students. This is the kind of "writing revolution" that increases satisfaction with teaching and learning, and it is the kind of writing instruction we hope this book will both serve and inspire.

Works Cited

Bartholomae, David. "Inventing the University." *When a Writer Can't Write: Studies in Writer's Block and Other Composing-Process Problems.* New York: Guildford, 1985. 134–65.

Bazerman, Charles. *Shaping Written Knowledge.* Madison: U of Wisconsin P, 1988.

Belluck, Pam. "Board for Kansas Deletes Evolution from Curriculum." *New York Times* 12 Aug. 1999.

Brereton, John C., ed. *The Origins of Composition Studies in the American College, 1875 1925.* Pittsburgh: U of Pittsburgh P, 1995.

Connolly, Paul, and Patricia Vilardi. *Writing to Learn Mathematics and Science.* New York: Teachers College P, 1989.

Connors, Robert J., and Andrea A. Lunsford. "Frequency of Formal Errors in Current College Writing, or Ma and Pa Kettle Do Research." *College Composition and Communication* 39 (1988): 395–409.

Elbow, Peter. "Inviting the Mother Tongue: Beyond 'Mistakes,' 'Bad English,' and 'Wrong Language.'" *Journal of Advanced Composition* 19 (1999): 359–88.

———. "The War between Reading and Writing — and How to End It." *Rhetoric Review* 12 (Fall 1993): 1–24.

Fakundiny, Lydia. Presentations and Handouts for Writing 700: Teaching Writing. Cornell U. Unpublished, 2001.

Freire, Paulo. *Pedagogy of the Oppressed.* 1970. New York: Continuum, 1986.

Gopen, George, and Judith Swan. "The Science of Scientific Writing." *American Scientist* 78 (1990): 550–58.

Gottschalk, Katherine. "Putting — and Keeping — the Cornell Writing Program in Its Place: Writing in the Disciplines." *Language and Learning across the Disciplines* 2.1 (1997): 22–45.

Hacker, Diana. *A Writer's Reference.* 5th ed. Boston: Bedford, 2003.

Henderson, David. *Experiencing Geometry.* Upper Saddle River: Prentice, 2001.

Lanham, Richard. *Revising Prose.* 4th ed. Boston: Allyn, 2000.

Light, Richard. *Making the Most of College: Students Speak Their Minds.* Cambridge: Harvard UP, 2001.

Lunsford, Andrea A. *The St. Martin's Handbook.* 5th ed. Boston: Bedford, 2003.

McKeachie, Wilbert. *Teaching Tips.* 8th ed. Lexington: Heath, 1986.

Monroe, Jonathan, ed. *Writing and Revising the Disciplines.* Ithaca: Cornell UP, 2002.

Monroe, Jonathan, ed. *Local Knowledges, Local Practices: Writing in the Disciplines at Cornell.* Pittsburgh: U of Pittsburgh P, 2003.

National Commission on Writing in America's Schools and Colleges. "The Neglected 'R': The Need for a Writing Revolution." Apr. 2003. College Board. http://www.writingcommission.org/prod_downloads/writingcom/neglectedr.pdf.

Paige, David, and Andrew Ingersoll. "Annual Heat Balance of Martian Polar Caps: Viking Observations." *Science* 228 (1985): 1160–68.

Pierpont, Judith. *Second Language Students in the Writing Class: A Manual for Instructors.* Rev. ed. Knight Inst.: Cornell U, 2001.

Pinker, Steven. *How the Mind Works.* New York: Norton, 1997.

Rowe, Mary Budd. "Wait Time: Slowing Down May Be Speeding Up." *Journal of Teacher Education* Jan.–Feb. 1986: 43–48.

Sommers, Nancy. "Responding to Student Writing." Harvard Writing Project Special Bulletin. Harvard U, 2000.

———. "Revision Strategies of Student Writers and Experienced Adult Writers." *College Composition and Communication.* 31 (1980) 378–88.

Trimble, John R. *Writing with Style: Conversations on the Art of Writing.* 2nd ed. Upper Saddle River, N.J.: Prentice, 2000.

Trosset, Carol. "Obstacles to Open Discussion and Critical Thinking." *Change* Sept.–Oct. 1998: 44–49.

Williams, Joseph. "On the Maturing of Legal Writers: Two Models of Growth and Development." 1991. *Legal Writing* 1:1–31.

Williams, Joseph, and Gregory G. Colomb. "The University of Chicago: Two Metaphors for Learning." *Programs That Work.* Ed. Toby Fulwiler and Art Young. Portsmouth: Boynton, 1990. 97–111.

———. "The Phenomenology of Error." *College Composition and Communication* 32 (1981): 152–68.

Index